Discrimination in Society

Racial Discrimination

Peggy J. Parks

ReferencePoint Press

San Diego, CA

About the Author

Peggy J. Parks holds a bachelor of science degree from Aquinas College in Grand Rapids, Michigan, where she graduated magna cum laude. An author who has written dozens of educational books on a wide variety of topics for teens and young adults, Parks lives in Muskegon, Michigan, a town she says inspires her writing because of its location on the shores of beautiful Lake Michigan.

Printed in the United States

For more information, contact:
ReferencePoint Press, Inc.
PO Box 27779
San Diego, CA 92198
www.ReferencePointPress.com

Picture Credits:

Cover: Elenabsl/Shutterstock.com
7: Maury Aaseng
11: Maury Aaseng
15: A segregated water fountain at Oklahoma City, 1939 (b/w photo), Lee, Russell (1903–86)/ Private Collection/Bridgeman Images
19: Everett collection/Newscom
23: Maury Aaseng
27: Aaron Josefczyk/Reuters/Newscom
30: ChameleonsEye/Shutterstock.com
35: Everett Collection/Newscom
38: Yoichi Okamoto/ZUMA Press/Newscom
46: Rob Marmion/Shutterstock.com
49: George Sheldon/Shutterstock.com
51: Arnie Sachs/MediaPunch/IPx
58: Associated Press
61: Maury Aaseng
64: Renee Jones Schneider/ZUMA Press/Newscom

LIBRARY OF CONGRESS CATALOGING-IN-PUBLICATION DATA

Name: Parks, Peggy J., 1951– author.
Title: Racial Discrimination/by Peggy J. Parks.
Description: San Diego, CA: ReferencePoint Press, Inc., [2019] | Series: Discrimination in Society | Includes bibliographical references and index. | Audience: Grades 9-12.
Identifiers: LCCN 2018003242 (print) | LCCN 2018015684 (ebook) | ISBN 9781682823866 (eBook) | ISBN 9781682823859 (hardback)
Subjects: LCSH: Race discrimination—United States—Juvenile literature. | Discrimination in law enforcement—United States—Juvenile literature. | Discrimination in housing—United States—Juvenile literature. | Discrimination in employment—United States—Juvenile literature. | Discrimination in education—United States—Juvenile literature. | Racism—United States—Juvenile literature.
Classification: LCC E184.A1 (ebook) | LCC E184.A1 P3264 2019 (print) | DDC 305.800973—dc23
LC record available at https://lccn.loc.gov/2018003242

CONTENTS

INTRODUCTION

Perspectives on Racial Discrimination

Something was very wrong in Flint, Michigan, during the spring of 2014. In an effort to save money, the city, which is about 60 percent African American, had changed its water source in late April. Residents started having problems almost immediately. The water coming out of their faucets was a reddish-brown color and foul smelling, and it tasted as bad as it smelled. Children and adults developed painful rashes on their skin, and many were also losing their hair. Some children developed more severe health issues, such as memory loss, dizziness, headaches, and convulsions. The residents of Flint were convinced that the water was causing these health problems.

A City in Crisis

Lee Anne Walters was one of many Flint residents who feared for her family's health. Her three-year-old twins broke out in rashes, and her teenage daughter panicked when clumps of hair fell out in the shower. Walters's teenage son developed headaches and abdominal pain, as well as a severe skin rash that burned when he took a bath or shower, causing him to cry out in pain.

Walters bought a testing kit to test her home's water. She was shocked to find that it contained alarmingly high levels of lead, which can cause profound, permanent health damage, especially to the brain and nervous system. She took her children to have blood tests and the results confirmed her worst fears. All four had been exposed to lead, and one of the twins had lead poisoning. She reported these issues to city officials more than once, but no one ever responded. The same was true for other Flint residents, whose pleas for help were ignored for more than a year. They showed up at city council meetings and were brushed off, even accused of lying about the water samples they brought with them.

> **"The levels [of lead] that we have seen in Flint are some of the worst that I have seen in more than 25 years working in the field."[1]**
>
> —Marc Edwards, a researcher from Virginia Polytechnic Institute and State University

In 2015 researchers from Virginia Polytechnic Institute and State University went to Flint and tested the water at dozens of homes. They found concentrations of lead that were hundreds of times higher than limits set by federal law. "The levels that we have seen in Flint are some of the worst that I have seen in more than 25 years working in the field,"[1] says researcher Marc Edwards. Subsequent research by a Flint pediatrician found dangerous lead levels in the bloodstreams of many Flint children.

How Could This Happen?

As news of the Flint water crisis spread, charges of discrimination were leveled at city officials and others who had made the decision to switch water sources and then ignored the concerns of residents. To address these claims, the Michigan Civil Rights Commission conducted an investigation and held public hearings. In February 2017 the commission released a scathing report, in which members declared that racial discrimination was absolutely at the root of the crisis in Flint. The report states, "The commission believes that we have answered our initial question, 'Was race a factor in the Flint Water Crisis?' Our answer is an unreserved and undeniable—'yes.'"[2]

A separate investigation that examined the city's new water source revealed aging and corroded pipes that had allowed lead to leach into the water supply. This problem, the Civil Rights Commission argues, would never have occurred in Michigan's wealthier white communities. "Would the Flint water crisis have been allowed to happen in Birmingham, Ann Arbor or East Grand Rapids?" the commission asks. "We believe the answer is no, and that the vestiges of segregation and discrimination found in Flint made it a unique target."[3]

Just One Example

Although the specific circumstances of the Flint water crisis were unique, how people in the largely black, low-income community were treated was not. At least, that is the perspective of many African Americans, civil rights groups, and other concerned individuals, who believe that what occurred in Flint was not an isolated incident. Rather, they view the Flint crisis as a microcosm of what is happening throughout the United States.

> **"We believe . . . that the vestiges of segregation and discrimination found in Flint made it a unique target."[3]**
>
> —Michigan Civil Rights Commission, which investigates the state's discrimination complaints

According to Anthony DiMaggio, assistant professor of political science at Lehigh University, there is a "mountain of statistical data showing American institutions treat citizens very differently based on race."[4] DiMaggio and other like-minded individuals believe this widespread racial discrimination is evident in numerous ways, from racial profiling and police brutality to being called racially offensive names at work or at school.

Different Viewpoints

Yet not everyone shares that view about racial discrimination. Although increasing numbers of Americans see racism as a major problem, they also have widely differing perceptions of how serious a problem it is. Surveys have shown that those perceptions differ significantly by race. In a February 2017 Public Religion Re-

More Americans Today See Racism as a Big Problem

The number of Americans who consider racism to be a big problem is growing. The percentage of Americans who feel this way rose 8 percent between 2015 and 2017 and more than doubled since 2011, according to a 2017 Pew Research Center article based on surveys conducted from 1995 to 2017.

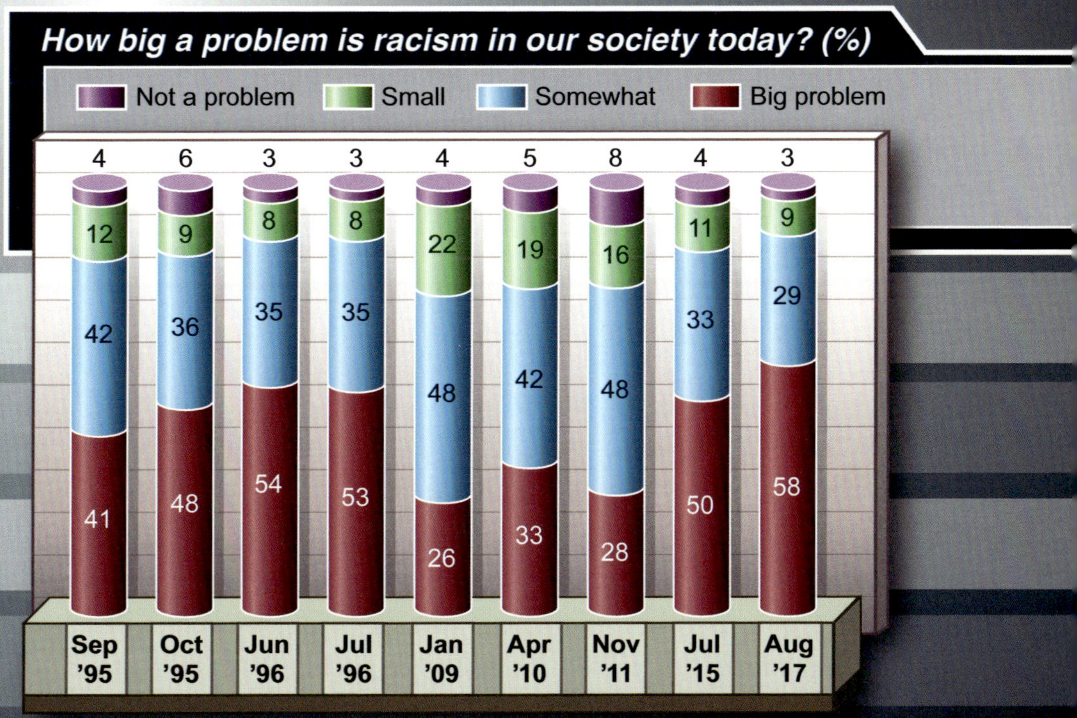

Source: Samantha Neal, "Views of Racism as a Major Problem Increase Sharply, Especially Among Democrats," Pew Research Center, August 29, 2017. www.pewresearch.org.

search Institute poll, for example, 87 percent of black respondents said that black people face a lot of discrimination in the United States. In contrast, only 49 percent of whites share that view about discrimination.

The institute's report closely parallels other surveys that have also found wide disparities in how people of different races view racial discrimination. One example is an August 2017 poll by the Pew Research Center, in which respondents were asked how big a problem racism is in American society today.

Of black respondents, 81 percent said racism is a big problem, compared with 52 percent of whites who said that.

Also in 2017, a Quinnipiac University poll asked about prejudice against minority groups in the United States. Among white respondents, only 39 percent viewed racial prejudice as a serious problem. This was in sharp contrast to nonwhite respondents, a group that included blacks, Hispanics, Asian Americans, Native Americans, and Pacific Islanders. When they were asked their views on racial prejudice, collectively 66 percent said it was a serious problem. "Public opinion polling paints a stark picture of wide disparities between African-Americans and other minorities compared to whites,"[5] says CNN Politics reporter and producer Ryan Struyk.

Racial Discrimination Is Real

Although people may not agree about the seriousness of racial discrimination, what happened in Flint, Michigan, is a striking example of its continued existence. When Americans are asked about it, their viewpoints typically depend on their race. Nonwhites, for example, tend to see racial discrimination as a more serious problem than whites do. As for whether people of different races will ever see this issue the same way, no one knows the answer.

CHAPTER 1

The Years-Long Struggle for Equality

Fourteen-year-old Taylissa Marriott could hardly wait for school to start in August 2017. She would be a freshman at Yerington High School in the small town of Yerington, Nevada. She planned to run cross-country and also to play basketball, confident that at nearly 6 feet (183 cm) tall she would be an asset to the team. Because of recognition for an essay she had written the year before, Taylissa had earned a place on the high school student council. She was ready and eager for the year to begin—but her enthusiasm soon turned to despair. Taylissa, who is black, encountered racial discrimination almost immediately after the school year began. "It's 2017," she says. "You would think racial stuff would be over, but it's not."[6]

Taunted and Threatened

Taylissa encountered racism nearly every day at school. A few students, such as a girl named C.T. and her group of friends, called Taylissa "nigger"[7] when they passed her in the hallway. On at least one occasion, a teacher standing nearby heard the racial slur and said nothing. In addition to calling her filthy names, the girls also blocked doorways so Taylissa could not get through as they taunted her and laughed at her. At a boys' volleyball game in mid-September 2017, Taylissa and her sister, Jayla, were sitting with a male classmate in the gymnasium. In a voice loud enough for everyone around them to hear,

C.T. said to the boy, "I thought you didn't like niggers."[8] Taylissa and Jayla were so upset they left the game and went home.

An occurrence the following month was the most frightening of all the racial incidents. On the evening of October 8, 2017, Taylissa and Jayla were at home in their room. They were notified by some friends about a white student's posts on Snapchat, so they got online and looked—and were horrified at what they saw. The photo showed the boy, who is the son of a sheriff's deputy, holding a gun and wearing a belt with knives, with the caption, "The redneck god of gods we about to go nigger huntin" superimposed over the photo. The caption of another photo of the same boy read: "Porch monkeys here I come."[9]

The photos shocked Taylissa and Jayla and frightened them badly. Their parents reported the incident to school officials, who minimized the seriousness of it. The sheriff's department was equally dismissive. They insisted that nothing could be done because no laws had been broken, and students who called the girls names were merely exercising their First Amendment rights. The harassment continued throughout the school year. Finally, in January 2018 the girls' parents filed a lawsuit against the school district and the city on behalf of their daughters. "It has just gotten out of hand," says Jayla. "When I saw the post I felt like we weren't wanted at school and it wasn't safe for us to go there because something was going to happen to us."[10]

Discrimination Sanctioned by Law

Racial discrimination is an ugly beast. No one should have to experience what Taylissa and Jayla have experienced. Being the target of discrimination is painful and stressful. When events like this occur, it is hard to believe that life for people of color has improved and that discrimination is less common and less vicious than it once was—but, overall, it is. During the late nineteenth and early twentieth centuries, white people were believed to be the superior race, and there was evidence of this belief virtually everywhere. By far, the worst conditions were found in

African Americans Say Racial Discrimination Is a Common Occurrence

Although progress has been made through the years, racial discrimination is an ongoing problem in the United States. African Americans who were surveyed between January and April 2017 say that discrimination affects many aspects of daily life, from employment-related issues to health care and voting.

Percent of African Americans Reporting Race-Related Discrimination in Specific Situations

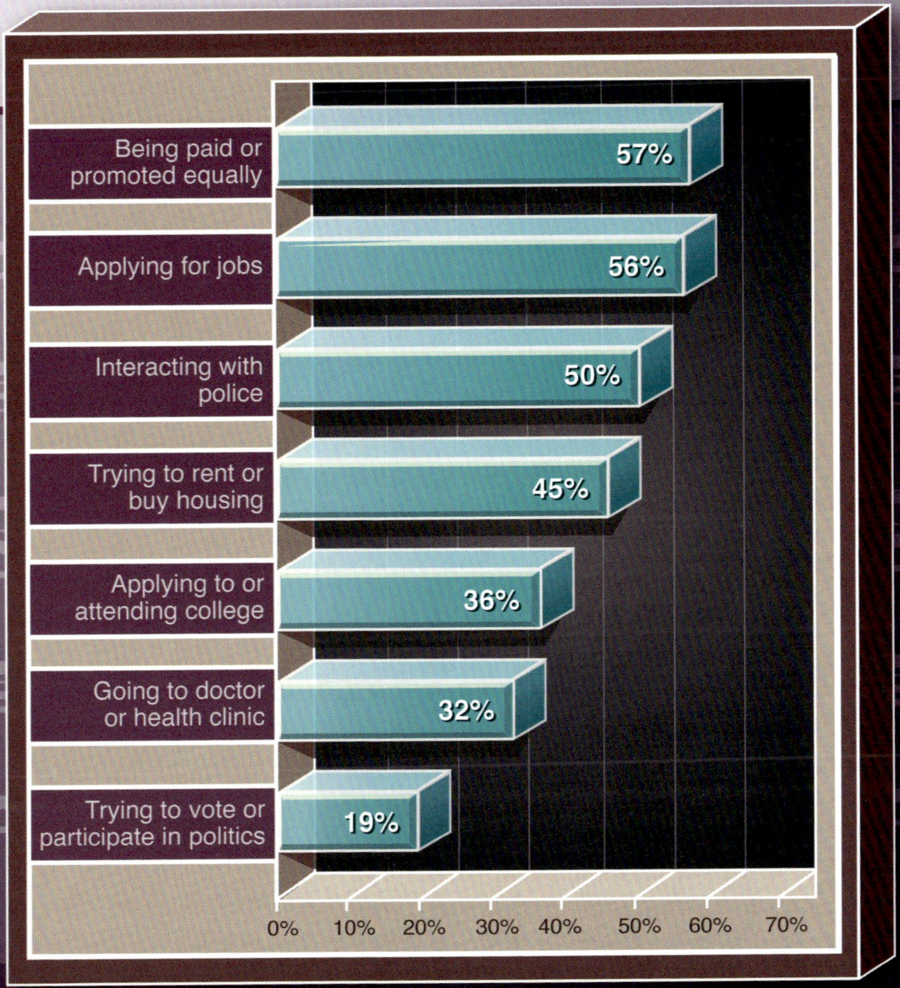

Source: National Public Radio, Robert Wood Johnson Foundation, and Harvard TH Chan School of Public Health, "Discrimination in America: Experiences and Views of African Americans," October 2017. www.npr.org.

the southern United States, where anger over the Civil War lingered for many years after the war ended in 1865. The Fourteenth Amendment to the Constitution had given all citizens—including African Americans—equal protection under the law. But a series of discriminatory laws and statutes passed by legislatures in the South denied people of color their civil rights and freedoms.

Collectively, these laws and statutes were known as Jim Crow, a mocking term that originated with a nineteenth-century minstrel song. Under this system, the laws to which people were subjected depended on their race—with people of color reduced to the status of second-class citizens. "Jim Crow was more than a series of rigid anti-black laws. It was a way of life,"[11] says Ferris State University sociology professor David Pilgrim. Jim Crow came to represent any state law passed in the South that established different sets of rules: one for whites and one for blacks. In 1890, for instance, the Louisiana General Assembly passed the Separate Car Law, which forbade black and white people from riding together in the same car on railroad trains.

In 1892 a biracial man named Homer A. Plessy challenged the Louisiana law by choosing a seat in the whites-only coach. He was ordered to leave the train and refused. As a result, Plessy was ejected, arrested, and jailed overnight. He hired an attorney to represent him but was found guilty of violating the law. He appealed the verdict. His case, known as *Plessy v. Ferguson*, went all the way to the US Supreme Court. In 1896 the court ruled that Louisiana's Separate Car Law would be allowed to stand. The justices declared that racial segregation did not necessarily represent an absence of equality, so it did not violate the Fourteenth Amendment.

"Jim Crow was more than a series of rigid anti-black laws. It was a way of life."[11]

—David Pilgrim, a sociology professor at Ferris State University

With this ruling, the justices established a new standard of racial separation, which came to be known as the doctrine of "separate but equal." Under this doctrine, businesses and public facilities could legally be designated for only blacks or only whites as long as the facilities were of equal quality. In practice, however,

A Courageous Little Girl

The 1954 Supreme Court ruling that outlawed racial segregation in American schools was largely ignored by southern states. Six years after the ruling, many schools in the South remained segregated. Finally, a federal judge in Louisiana gave that state's schools an integration deadline of November 14, 1960. For a little black girl from New Orleans named Ruby Nell Bridges, the ruling meant she could finally attend a school close to her home. No longer would she have to travel several miles to attend kindergarten at the all-black school.

When the day arrived, Ruby and her mother rode in a black limousine with federal marshals. The judge had anticipated that white people would protest, so he sent the marshals to protect Ruby. Sure enough, at the school they were met by a large, shouting mob of white people who were screaming obscenities, waving their fists, and throwing things. Surrounded by the big, protective men, Ruby made history when she and her mother walked past the crowd and into the all-white school. One of the marshals, Charles Burks, remembers that day well. "For a little girl six years old going into a strange school with four strange deputy marshals, a place she had never been before, she showed a lot of courage," he says. "She never cried. She didn't whimper. She just marched along like a little soldier. We were all very proud of her."

Quoted in Toby Mac and Michael Tait, "In a Class of Only One: Ruby Bridges," CBN, 2004. www.cbn.com.

facilities available to blacks were rarely of equal quality to the facilities for whites. This ruling, according to Pilgrim, sent an implicit but clear message to the states: "Discrimination against blacks is acceptable."[12]

The Jim Crow system affected virtually every aspect of black people's lives. Many of these laws severely restricted and/or forbade social interactions between people of different races. In South Carolina, for instance, black and white textile workers were forbidden from working in the same room, going in or out the same doors, or even looking out the same windows. An ordinance in Birmingham, Alabama, made it illegal for blacks and whites to play checkers or dominoes together. The state of Oklahoma passed a law forbidding people of different races to go boating together. Throughout the South, signs above drinking fountains and door entrances and in front of public facilities clearly designated "White" and "Colored." Pilgrim writes:

> There were separate hospitals for blacks and whites, separate prisons, separate public and private schools, separate churches, separate cemeteries, separate public restrooms, and separate public accommodations. In most instances, the black facilities were grossly inferior—generally, older, less-well-kept. In other cases, there were no black facilities—no Colored public restroom, no public beach, no place to sit or eat. *Plessy* gave Jim Crow states a legal way to ignore their constitutional obligations to their black citizens.[13]

Under Jim Crow, black people lived in fear for their lives. If they dared to violate any of the laws or rules of etiquette, they risked severe punishment. White people could legally beat black people, and they were often encouraged, rather than stopped. "Violence was instrumental for Jim Crow," says Pilgrim. "It was a method of social control."[14] The most extreme and violent forms of violence under the Jim Crow system were known as lynchings. These were public murders, usually hangings, carried out by mobs of angry white people.

Discrimination in the North

Even though Jim Crow laws and statutes were unique to the southern states, people of color also faced widespread discrimination in the North. During the early 1900s, a time known as the Great Migration, millions of African Americans fled the South and settled in northern states. By 1920 at least 1 million black people had moved north. Many of these people settled in large cities such as Philadelphia, Detroit, Chicago, and New York City. As the black population grew in these areas, white people became resentful over the competition for jobs, as well as living space in cities that had grown increasingly more crowded. Segregation became nearly as commonplace in the North as it had in the South. After World War II, which ended in 1945, northern cities became even more segregated. In a phenomenon known as white flight, white people moved out of cities and settled in the suburbs, where black people were clearly not welcome.

By the mid-twentieth century, New York City had become one of the North's most segregated cities. This was apparent most everywhere, from neighborhoods and schools to public accommodations. One African American man related his experience during the 1950s in an interview with a civil rights group: "Every time I'm downtown I see invisible signs on the door of every restaurant, saying 'Negroes, Keep out!' I make up my mind to have

A young man drinks from the water cooler designated for African Americans at a train terminal in Oklahoma in 1939. Throughout the South, buildings clearly designated separate bathrooms and drinking fountains for black people.

a good meal, and I walk for blocks, looking at every eating place I see, and wondering. . . . And then I get cold feet and end up at a cafeteria—or else get a sandwich in a drug store."[15] This experience was not unusual for black people in many other northern cities. Throughout the United States, rampant racial discrimination was a fact of life.

A Pivotal Ruling

Education is one example of how widespread segregation was in the early 1950s. Over one-third of the states had segregated schools, including both northern and southern states. Although all schools were supposed to be equal under *Plessy v. Ferguson*, black schools fell far short of being equal to white schools. One major contributor to this inequality was funding. In the South,

The Woolworth's Lunch Counter Protest

The Woolworth's discount store in Greensboro, North Carolina, was a lot like other businesses in the South in the 1950s. Its popular lunch counter had a strict whites-only policy. On February 1, 1960, four black college students decided to challenge that policy. They walked in, sat down on stools at the counter, and ordered coffee. The shocked waitresses, who were white, ignored the men, and the store manager asked them to leave. They refused to do so. For the rest of the day, they sat on the stools and did not leave until the store was closing for the evening.

The four young men returned the following day, accompanied by more black students. This continued over the next several months, with the group of young African Americans growing larger and larger. When the media learned about the sit-in, reporters and photographers arrived at Woolworth's to capture it in news stories. The four men became known as the Greensboro Four. Heavy television coverage spread awareness of their protest, and over the next few weeks this sparked a movement that spread to college towns throughout the United States. These grassroots protests contributed to the end of segregation in many dining facilities—including the Greensboro Woolworth's. By the end of July 1960, the store quietly opened its lunch counter to all patrons, regardless of race.

black schools received only about 60 percent of the funding allocated for white schools.

In 1954 the Supreme Court issued a ruling that eventually paved the way toward equality in schools. The case, known as *Brown v. Board of Education*, came into being after lower courts repeatedly denied attempts to do away with school segregation. With the *Brown* ruling, which was unanimous, the justices declared that the *Plessy v. Ferguson* ruling should be overturned.

> **"We conclude that, in the field of public education, the doctrine of 'separate but equal' has no place. Separate educational facilities are inherently unequal."[16]**
>
> —Earl Warren, former chief justice of the US Supreme Court

"We conclude that, in the field of public education, the doctrine of 'separate but equal' has no place," Chief Justice Earl Warren stated. "Separate educational facilities are inherently unequal." Warren went on to state that separating children from others of similar age and qualifications solely because of their race "generates a feeling of inferiority as to their status in the community that may affect their hearts and minds in a way unlikely ever to be undone."[16] In a separate ruling the following year, the justices ordered that states desegregate their schools as quickly as possible.

School integration did not happen quickly, despite the Supreme Court ruling. For many years afterward, schools throughout the United States remained segregated. But *Brown v. Board of Education* proved to be an important step toward ending racial discrimination.

Taking a Stand

Beyond school segregation, the Supreme Court addressed other types of inequalities during the 1950s, such as in public transportation. In the years following *Plessy v. Ferguson*, laws in the South required black people who rode buses to sit in designated "colored sections" in the back. Even when they were seated in those sections, they had to give up their seats if the white sections were full and white people needed seats. This policy led to a now-famous act of defiance by an African American woman from Montgomery, Alabama. Her name was Rosa Parks.

In December 1955, after working a long day as a seamstress, Parks was bone tired. As she boarded her bus, all she could think about was getting home. She sat in the appropriate section, and after a few stops several white people got on. The white section was full, and one white man was left standing, so the driver demanded that Parks give him her seat. She refused. Soon two police officers boarded the bus, arrested her, and took her away in a squad car. "I didn't feel good about going to jail," she later said, "but I was willing to go to let it be known that under this type of segregation, black people had endured too much for too long."[17]

When Parks refused to give up her bus seat for a white passenger, she had no idea what a far-reaching effect her action would have. Her bravery sparked a massive civil uprising known as the Montgomery Bus Boycott. For 381 days black people in Montgomery—more than forty-thousand of them—stopped riding buses. Since African Americans represented about 75 percent of bus ridership, the boycott caused a huge economic loss for the bus company. In November 1956, in the case of *Browder v. Gayle*, the Supreme Court ruled that bus segregation was illegal. The following month the boycott ended. Once again African Americans began riding buses, but they sat wherever they chose to sit.

The Civil Rights Movement

The bus boycott and other actions sparked nonviolent protests throughout the United States during the early 1960s. During this time a young African American man named Martin Luther King Jr. emerged as a leader in the up-and-coming civil rights movement. King, who was a Baptist minister, had served as president of the Southern Christian Leadership Conference. He believed in the importance of nonviolent, peaceful protest. "In the process of gain-

A black woman named Rosa Parks was arrested for refusing to give up her seat on a bus for a white male passenger in 1955. She is seen here after her arrest being fingerprinted by a sheriff in Montgomery, Alabama.

ing our rightful place, we must not be guilty of wrongful deeds," King said. "Let us not seek to satisfy our thirst for freedom by drinking from the cup of bitterness and hatred. We must not allow our creative protest to degenerate into physical violence."[18]

On August 28, 1963, King led a massive protest march in Washington, DC, known as the March on Washington for Jobs and Freedom. An estimated 250,000 people, both black and white, took part in the march, which began at the Washington Monument and ended at the Lincoln Memorial. Participants joined together to show solidarity and to emphasize their belief in equality for all citizens regardless of race. It was during this march, in front of the Lincoln Memorial, that King gave his "I Have a Dream" speech, in which he discussed his vision of everyone being equal regardless of race. "Even though we face the difficulties of today

"I have a dream that one day this nation will rise up and live out the true meaning of its creed: 'We hold these truths to be self-evident: that all men are created equal.'"[19]

—Martin Luther King Jr., a leader of the civil rights movement

and tomorrow, I still have a dream," King said. "It is a dream deeply rooted in the American dream. I have a dream that one day this nation will rise up and live out the true meaning of its creed: 'We hold these truths to be self-evident: that all men are created equal.'"[19]

The march on Washington played a major role in the growth of the civil rights movement in the United States. The 1960s brought some major legislative victories for African Americans, including the Civil Rights Act of 1964 and the Voting Rights Act of 1965. King continued to play a critical role in the movement until his death on April 4, 1968. Just hours after giving another famous speech, "I've Been to the Mountaintop," King was shot and killed as he stood on the balcony of his hotel room in Memphis, Tennessee.

Moving Forward

Five decades have passed since King's death, and much progress has been made toward his dream of equality. But people of color still face many hurdles and do not always enjoy the same rights and privileges as white people. During a July 2016 speech in Dallas, Texas, America's first African American president, Barack Obama, touched on this issue. "Race relations have improved dramatically in my lifetime," he said. "Those who deny it are dishonoring the struggles that helped us achieve that progress." Yet Obama also made it clear that since racial discrimination had existed for centuries, it was not going to vanish overnight because laws were passed to make it illegal. "America, we know that bias remains," Obama said. "We know it. . . . And while some suffer far more under racism's burden, some feel to a far greater extent discrimination's sting."[20]

CHAPTER 2

Law Enforcement

In recent years a surge of news coverage in the United States has focused on police shootings of unarmed black males. Civil rights advocates and many other members of the general public have grown increasingly alarmed by the number of shootings and the role racial discrimination seems to have played in them. But in order to fully understand why these shootings are happening, it is necessary to examine the data behind them—and thus far, such data has been practically nonexistent.

Digging for the Truth

Information on police shootings is difficult to find. No single government agency is charged with keeping track of this information, nor are police departments required to furnish the data to any other agency. To fill this information gap, activists, volunteer researchers, and media organizations have taken it on themselves to pull together data from news reports and other sources.

One media organization that has taken a leadership role in this research is the *Washington Post*. Since 2015, reporters from the *Post* have compiled and entered into a database information about every fatal police shooting in the United States. The newspaper's investigation has found that nearly one thousand police killings occurred each year for three years in a row, during the years 2015, 2016, and 2017. The statistics show that a disproportionate number of the dead were black or Hispanic. In terms of actual numbers, more whites were killed by police than people of color. But non-Hispanic whites represent about 62 percent of the US population, whereas blacks are slightly over 13 percent, and Hispanics are 18 percent. When adjusting for these population differences, African Americans and Hispanics were killed by police far more often than whites.

The findings of the *Post* investigations were nearly identical to the results of a December 2016 study by James W. Buehler. A health management and policy professor at Drexel University in Philadelphia, Pennsylvania, Buehler analyzed national statistics and census data from 2010 to 2014. Of the 2,285 fatal encounters with police officers over that period of time, black men were nearly three times as likely as white men to be killed by police officers. Hispanic men were nearly twice as likely as whites to be killed. In his published report Buehler states that "substantial racial-ethnic disparities" in fatal shootings by police officers "remain an ongoing problem in the United States."[21]

A Senseless Killing

One of these shootings occurred on April 29, 2017, and left a fifteen-year-old black youth dead. Jordan Edwards was a popular honors student from Balch Springs, Texas, who played on his high school football team. On Saturday, April 29, he and his two older brothers finished their chores at home and asked their dad if they could go to a party. He said yes, as long as they agreed not to drink alcohol and to be home by midnight. The boys agreed and hopped into their dad's black Chevy Impala with two of their friends. Jordan's brother Vidal drove to the party at a house a few miles away.

About an hour after the boys arrived, two white police officers showed up at the home. They had been dispatched after neighbors complained about excessive noise and kids blocking driveways with cars. Anticipating that there might be trouble, Vidal rounded up his group and told them they needed to leave. They climbed in the car, with Vidal at the wheel, Jordan in the front passenger seat, and the other three boys in back. As they

Police and Public Have Different Views on Shootings

In 2016 the Pew Research Center surveyed police officers and the general public to gauge their attitudes toward fatal encounters between police officers and African Americans. When asked whether these deaths were isolated incidents or signs of a broader problem, the two groups gave very different answers.

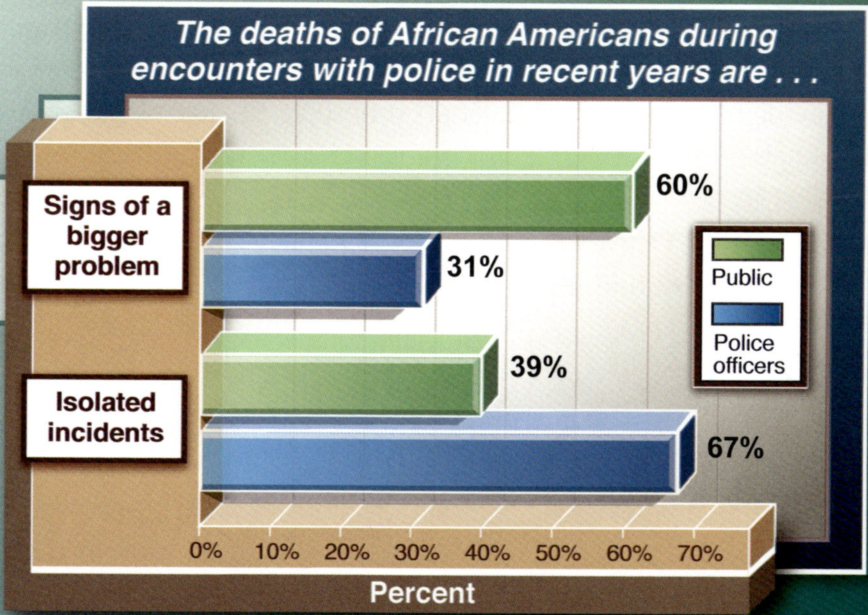

Source: Rich Morin et al., "Behind the Badge," Pew Research Center, January 11, 2017. www.pewsocialtrends.org.

pulled away, one of the officers, Roy Oliver, yelled at them to stop the car. Vidal, who heard yelling but did not know it was directed at him, kept driving. Oliver reached into his patrol car, grabbed a rifle, and opened fire on the carload of teens.

Bullets tore through the passenger window and struck Jordan in the head. He slumped over, bleeding heavily from the wounds, while his brothers and friends stared in shock and horror. As soon as Vidal stopped the car, Oliver and his partner yanked open the doors and put handcuffs on the four uninjured teens. Vidal later said the officers barked orders at him, telling him to get out of the car and walk to the left. He moved right by mistake and heard one of the officers say: "This nigger doesn't know his . . . left from his right."[22] Medical personnel arrived and transported Jordan to a nearby hospital, where he was pronounced dead.

The Dallas County medical examiner ruled Jordan's death a homicide caused by a rifle wound to the head. Within days Oliver was fired from his job, arrested, and charged with aggravated assault with a deadly weapon and murder. During a press conference to announce the charges, Dallas County district attorney Faith Johnson said the decision to charge the officer represented "a message we're sending to bad police officers. And that is, if you do wrong, we will prosecute you."[23]

> **"How many black men have to die before law enforcement changes its culture and regains the trust of the communities it's sworn to serve?"[24]**
>
> —Terri Burke, an executive with the American Civil Liberties Union

Jordon's family and civil rights advocates believe that racial bias was to blame for his death. "How many black men have to die before law enforcement changes its culture and regains the trust of the communities it's sworn to serve?"[24] asks Terri Burke, an executive with the American Civil Liberties Union. Oliver's trial was set to begin in June 2018. If convicted, he faced a possible sentence of several life terms in prison.

Vastly Different Viewpoints

According to polls, many Americans believe that police officers are more likely to shoot black suspects than white suspects. The view from inside law enforcement is very different. In a January 2017 Pew Research Center survey, 60 percent of people in the general public said police shootings are signs of a broader problem, rather than isolated incidents. Opinions by police officers were virtually the opposite, with 67 percent saying the killings were isolated incidents, rather than signs of a broader problem.

Police perspectives, however, varied by race. Of white police officers, 72 percent believed the deaths of blacks during encounters with police were isolated incidents. Among black police of-

Walking While Black

African Americans throughout the United States report that police discriminate against them in numerous ways, such as ticketing them for alleged violations far more often than white people are ticketed. Because this happens not only when blacks are driving but also while they are walking, they have colloquially termed it "walking while black." One community where this was shown to be a problem is Jacksonville, Florida. The sheriff's office issues hundreds of pedestrian tickets each year. According to an analysis by the nonprofit news organization ProPublica, these tickets are issued to blacks three times more often than to whites. The majority of tickets are issued to young black males aged fourteen to thirty-five.

One of those young black men is Michael Anderson. In April 2016 he left his mother's home in Jacksonville and started walking to a grocery store. Three police officers approached him and told him they had seen him jaywalk. They asked for identification and attempted to search him. Anderson balked at that, and they threatened to put him in handcuffs for resisting arrest. "Why are you all bothering me?" he asked them. "You're only harassing me because I'm a black male, with dreads in this high crime area." The officers ticketed Anderson for what they said was walking in a roadway where sidewalks are provided. He went to court to contest the citation. When none of the officers showed up at the hearing, the citation was dismissed.

Quoted in Topher Sanders et al., "Walking While Black," ProPublica, November 16, 2017. www.propublica.org.

ficers, just 43 percent believed the killings were isolated incidents, with most saying this was a sign of a bigger problem.

Redditt Hudson is a former police officer from St. Louis, Missouri, who views the shootings of black citizens as a societal problem. Referring to himself as a "black ex-cop," Hudson left law enforcement in 1999 largely because of what he saw as system-wide racial discrimination. "Institutional racism runs through our criminal justice system," says Hudson. "Its presence in police culture, though often flatly denied by the many police apologists that appear in the media now, has been central to the

> **"Institutional racism runs through our criminal justice system."[25]**
>
> —Redditt Hudson, a former police officer from St. Louis, Missouri

breakdown in police-community relationships for decades in spite of good people doing police work."[25]

Hudson cites an incident in Cleveland, Ohio, that occurred on November 29, 2012. It involved two unarmed black people, Timothy Russell and Malissa Williams. Russell's Chevrolet Malibu backfired, and police officers mistook the sounds for gunshots. A chase ensued that lasted for more than twenty minutes, wound throughout the city, and involved sixty-two police cars. When Russell finally pulled to a stop, thirteen officers opened fire, shooting at least 137 rounds into the car. Officer Michael Brelo, who is white, fired forty-nine of the rounds and continued firing even after the perceived threat had ended. At one point Brelo climbed onto the hood of the car and shot fifteen rounds through the windshield, striking both Russell and Williams. He was charged with their deaths, and at his trial in 2015 was acquitted of all charges. This verdict in the Cleveland courtroom outraged civil rights advocates, who were convinced that racial discrimination was at the root of the shooting.

Scathing Federal Reports

The Cleveland Division of Police (CDP) was one of several dozen law enforcement agencies investigated by the US Department of Justice (DOJ). In a 2014 report of the Cleveland investigation, the DOJ explained that tactics used by the police department were contributing to the community's distrust and lack of respect for police. Officers were drawing their guns on people suspected of minor crimes or who did not otherwise pose a threat, as well as stopping people without any reasonable suspicion of wrongdoing.

Although the investigation did not find concrete evidence of racial discrimination, black Cleveland residents reported that they were regularly discriminated against by police. The DOJ states:

> We must report that when we interviewed members of the community about their experiences with the police, many African-Americans reported that they believe CDP officers are verbally and physically aggressive toward them because of their race. We also found that, when community members attempt to file complaints about mistreatment at the hands of CDP officers, they are met with barriers and resistance.[26]

Another city whose police department was investigated by the DOJ was Ferguson, Missouri. The investigation was triggered by an incident that occurred on August 9, 2014. A white police officer named Darren Wilson shot and killed an unarmed African American teenager named Michael Brown. Wilson justified his actions, saying he felt threatened by Brown and had shot the teen in self-defense. But several witnesses told a different story. One of them was Brown's friend, Dorian Johnson. "I saw the officer proceeding after my friend Big Mike with his gun drawn, and he fired a second shot and that struck my friend," says Johnson. "And at

In 2012 two unarmed black suspects were shot dead in their car (pictured) by police who fired at least 137 rounds into the car. A police officer was charged with manslaughter for the killings but was later acquitted.

that time, he turned around with his hands up, beginning to tell the officer that he was unarmed and to tell him to stop shooting. But at that time, the officer fired several more shots into my friend, and he hit the ground and died."[27]

On November 25, 2014, a grand jury announced that there was insufficient evidence to indict Wilson for a crime. The city of Ferguson erupted into chaos, and massive protests stretched on for weeks. This served as a catalyst not only for the DOJ investigations but also for a national debate on the use of excessive force by police officers in the course of doing their jobs.

In its March 2015 report of what happened in Ferguson, the DOJ stated that the city's approach to law enforcement reflected

An Unconstitutional Police Practice

For many years police departments in cities throughout the United States used a practice known as "stop and frisk." Under this practice, police had the authority to stop anyone, at any time, if they suspected the person was in the process of committing a crime, had already committed a crime, or was about to commit a crime. Officers could ask questions, and if the situation seemed to warrant it, could frisk the person. This policy was a target of frequent criticism because police were found to be using it to discriminate against people of color. A study of New York City, for example, found that from 2004 to 2014 nearly 4.5 million police stops were made, and 83 percent involved blacks or Hispanics. These numbers raised concerns since blacks and Hispanics together account for just over half of the city's population.

In 2013 a federal judge ruled that New York City's stop and frisk policy was unconstitutional. She discussed how police officers often stopped young minority men for no apparent reason, frisked them for weapons, and/or searched them for contraband. This, the judge stated, was not only discriminatory, it violated the Constitution's Fourth Amendment. In her closing remarks, she said, "No one should live in fear of being stopped whenever he leaves his home to go about the activities of daily life."

Quoted in Bernard Vaughan, "NYPD's 'Stop-and-Frisk' Practice Unconstitutional, Judge Rules," Reuters, August 12, 2013. www.reuters.com.

and reinforced racial bias, including stereotyping. "The harms of Ferguson's police and court practices are borne disproportionately by African Americans," says the DOJ, "and there is evidence that this is due in part to intentional discrimination on the basis of race."[28] The report also pointed out that Ferguson police officers were quick to escalate force—and when they did, it involved African Americans at least 90 percent of the time.

Racial Profiling

Investigations by the DOJ have also revealed a high prevalence of racial profiling in many US cities, including Ferguson. Racial profiling occurs when people are singled out by law enforcement solely because of their race. In Ferguson, for instance, the DOJ found that from 2012 to 2014, black people accounted for 85 percent of traffic stops, 90 percent of citations, and 93 percent of arrests made by police. In addition, black citizens were twice as likely as whites to be searched during a traffic stop. "Racial profiling is a form of discrimination that is not only despicable, but also is an illegal and improper basis for any police officer to stop, search, arrest or investigate another person,"[29] says criminal defense attorney and CNN legal consultant Mark NeJame.

Surveys have shown that when people of color have experienced racial profiling, a natural reaction is for them to distrust police officers. This can lead to ongoing strife between police departments and the communities they are sworn to serve. To better understand the significance of this problem, National Public Radio and partner groups conducted a survey in 2017. More than three thousand people eighteen years of age and older participated by sharing their own personal experiences with discrimination, including by law enforcement.

Sixty percent of African Americans said they had, at some point in their lives, been unfairly stopped or treated badly by police because of their race. Black people also reported going out of their way to minimize potential interactions with police. For instance,

Police in San Francisco talk with a young black man. Surveys have shown that when people of color have experienced racial profiling, a natural reaction is to distrust the police.

31 percent said they had avoided calling the police even when in need because they feared they would be discriminated against. Similarly, 27 percent of African Americans said they had avoided certain activities, such as driving a car or participating in social or political events, in order to avoid potentially interacting with police. "African-Americans do not have a high level of trust in the police," says Elizabeth Hinton, assistant professor of history and of African and African American studies at Harvard University. "More than a

quarter avoid doing ordinary activities due to fear of coming into contact with them."[30]

Excessive Force

In communities where racial profiling is a serious problem, people of color often report being treated roughly by police. In fact, research has shown that nonwhite citizens (particularly blacks) are more likely to be subjected to violent treatment by police than white citizens. "Black suspects are more likely to be pushed against a wall, handcuffed without being arrested, pushed to the ground, pepper sprayed, touched by hand, or had a weapon drawn on them,"[31] says Anthony DiMaggio, assistant professor of political science at Lehigh University.

> **"African-Americans do not have a high level of trust in the police."[30]**
>
> —Elizabeth Hinton, assistant professor of history and of African and African American studies at Harvard University

In its report on Ferguson, the DOJ notes that police have used a disproportionate amount of force against black people compared with white people. Nearly 90 percent of documented force used by the city's police officers was found to be against African Americans. This included using police dogs to bite people, including children, in situations where such excessive force was uncalled for. And in every police dog biting incident for which racial information was reported, the person bitten was black. The DOJ states that the Ferguson Police Department's "use of dog bites only against African-American subjects is evidence of discriminatory policing in violation of the Fourteenth Amendment and other federal laws."[32]

Police departments in numerous US cities have been criticized and investigated for using excessive force against black citizens. One of these is in Chicago, Illinois. Based on an investigation of law enforcement data, the DOJ concluded that Chicago police officers used force nearly ten times more often with black suspects than with white suspects. From 2011 to 2016 African Americans in Chicago were the target of 80 percent of police firearm uses and 81 percent of all Taser and/or stun gun uses. In situations in which police used force against a minor, 83 percent were black children and 14 percent were Hispanic children. The DOJ writes:

> Chicago's black and Latino communities live not only with higher crime, but also with more instances of police abuse. Starting from a young age, black and Latino people, especially those living in Chicago's most challenged neighborhoods, have a vastly different experience with police than do white people. These negative, often tragic, interactions form the basis of minority communities' distrust of police.[33]

A Troubling Situation

Evidence is compelling that the experience many African Americans have with law enforcement differs from that of white people. Investigations by criminologists, the news media, and the DOJ have revealed a disturbing prevalence of excessive force (including shootings), racial profiling, and rough treatment of black citizens compared with whites. Criminal justice experts and civil rights advocates hope that by bringing these situations to light, much-needed changes in law enforcement can be made. "We need police officers," says Hudson. "We also need them to be held accountable to the communities they serve."[34]

CHAPTER 3

Housing Discrimination

In the fall of 2016, shortly after Gustavo Douaihi and Laura Smith were married, they saw a house for rent in Baton Rouge, Louisiana. Douaihi, a geologist from Venezuela, and Smith, a high school English teacher from Alabama, had been renting a tiny house and were feeling a bit cramped. The new place was in the same neighborhood where they had been living, but it was bigger and nicer. Douaihi called the number on the For Rent sign. He left a voice message with his name and phone number and explained that he and his wife were interested in looking at the house. When no one responded to his message after a week, Douaihi called again and left the same message. Again, there was no reply.

So Smith decided to give it a try. She called the number and left a similar voice message, along with what she later described as her "very white" name. She received a text from the landlord within five minutes. "It was so clear that the landlord responded differently to me than to my husband," she says. "The only different information she had between the two voicemails was . . . a Hispanic name."[35]

Subtle Discrimination

If indeed the landlord discriminated against Douaihi because he is Hispanic, she was breaking the law. Discrimination based on race or skin color, national origin, religion, sex, disability, or familial status is illegal under the Fair Housing Act. Anyone who rents or sells houses or apartments or works with people to obtain financing for such dwellings cannot discriminate against people for any of these reasons. Violating the law can have severe repercussions, including tens of thousands of dollars in fines and other associated costs.

Despite the law and penalties, housing discrimination happens more often than many people realize. This is true all over the United States. One person who experienced it is Danielle Douglas-Gabriel, a black journalist who writes for the *Washington Post*. She was unprepared for what she encountered while searching for her first home along with her husband, who is a university history professor and also black. They were relocating from Washington, DC, to Connecticut and were excited because for the first time since they married, they could afford to buy their own home. They attended several open houses in what turned out to be predominantly white neighborhoods. The reception they got was distressing. "It wasn't anything that anyone said," says Douglas-Gabriel, "but the looks from neighbors as my husband and I went to one showing after another conveyed the message: What are you doing here?"[36]

When Housing Discrimination Was Legal

The message would not have been as subtle in the 1950s and earlier, when African Americans were not allowed to even consider buying homes in white neighborhoods. Federal and state laws actually *protected* those who discriminated against people of color, and housing discrimination was rampant and widespread. In the early to mid-twentieth century, segregation was sanctioned by formal and legally enforceable agreements known as covenants.

Restrictive covenants were often part of deeds that designated property ownership. They controlled how property could be developed and used, as well as who could buy or rent the property. "A covenant was a private contract between property owners within a specific geographic area who agreed not to rent or sell homes to African Americans," says Princeton University sociologist Douglas S. Massey. "Once a majority of property own-

Police and white citizens gather in the street as a black family moves into a neighborhood in the 1950s. During this period, laws protected whites who engaged in housing discrimination.

ers in a covered area had signed the covenant, it became binding and violators could be sued in court for breach of contract."[37] By the mid-twentieth century, segregation had become the norm in major cities throughout the United States. If integrated neighborhoods existed in these cities, they were extremely rare.

Housing discrimination flourished with the help of federal, state, and local governments. Buy-in from the real estate industry also contributed to the longevity of discrimination in housing. In fact, real estate agents were a powerful force in keeping neighborhoods segregated. As one real estate agent opined in the 1950s, "It's a sort of unwritten code that respectable real estate brokers should guide people into the areas where they'll fit in socially and keep them out of areas where they won't. Everybody's happier that way. The people who live in the neighborhood are happier.

The customers are happier, in the long run. And as for the broker himself, he's happier—it's good business to fit people in."[38]

Unscrupulous Practices

Many people who worked in real estate in the mid-twentieth century were simply doing their jobs within the confines of a system that fostered racial discrimination. But some actively tried to take advantage of home buyers and sellers by exploiting people's fears. These unethical agents were known as panic peddlers or blockbusters. They scoured communities to identify white neighborhoods that bordered on low-income black neighborhoods. Then they approached white home owners and launched into a spiel that was intended to scare them into selling their homes. Panic peddlers warned the home owners that the neighborhood was about to go downhill. They said that black people were rapidly moving close by and this would surely cause white property values to plummet. The agents offered to buy the homes at prices that were far less than they were worth, but they sweetened the deal by paying cash. Fearing that their major investment was at risk, many white home owners were scared into accepting these offers.

> **"It's a sort of unwritten code that respectable real estate brokers should guide people into the areas where they'll fit in socially and keep them out of areas where they won't."[38]**
>
> —An unnamed real estate agent in the 1950s

Once the houses had been vacated, the agents grossly inflated the selling prices. Then they sought out African Americans who were eager to own their own homes. Because blacks could not usually obtain mortgages, the agents provided land contracts with extraordinarily high interest rates and questionable terms. Panic peddlers were reviled by people from all walks of life. A 1998 *Fordham Law Review* paper explains, "Whites hated them for dismantling their cozy neighborhoods, progressives hated them for harming blacks, and newspaper and government reports blamed them for destroying neighborhoods and fostering racial tension."[39]

Another dishonest practice that was common during the early to mid-twentieth century was known as *redlining*. A term coined by sociologist and civil rights advocate John McKnight, redlining refers to deliberate attempts to keep people of color from buying or renting in certain neighborhoods. Specifically, it describes a discriminatory practice that was used by banks when determining loan eligibility. They did not want to loan money to African Americans, so they mapped out a plan—literally.

Loan officers kept large maps that showed a community's neighborhoods. To indicate where they were not willing to loan money for property (such as black neighborhoods in inner cities), loan officers used red markers to draw lines around these areas.

A Demoralizing Experience

When Jenn M. Jackson and her husband decided to put their home up for sale, they were confident it would sell quickly. It was located in a lovely, predominantly white neighborhood in Orange County, California, where comparable homes sold within weeks of being listed. To increase their home's appeal, they made small repairs, freshened paint, and packed away unused items to reduce clutter. They moved out excess furniture to create a feeling of spaciousness. They even bought new artwork for the walls. "We were certain it would only be on the market for a month at most," says Jackson. But they were wrong.

People attended open houses or came to look at the house with real estate agents, but no one made an offer. Finally the Jacksons, who are African American, concluded that potential buyers did not want to live in a house that had been home to a black family. Only when they put away everything that could possibly reveal their race and left all interaction to the real estate agent did the house finally sell—for a price significantly lower than similar houses in the neighborhood. "The only discernible difference," says Jackson, "was the race of the occupants." She and her husband suffered financially and emotionally. "Our experiences showed us that while we could change everything about our home, we couldn't change the color of our skin, nor the stigma attached to it."

Jenn M. Jackson, "How 'Selling a Home While Black' Nearly Broke Me," *Root*, February 4, 2015. www.theroot.com.

Referring to Chicago, Illinois, and Milwaukee, Wisconsin, which were notorious cities for redlining, attorney Dean Browning Webb writes, "Mortgage lenders literally drew red lines around minority areas and instructed loan officers to deny any mortgage applications inside the areas so marked. Lenders, real estate agents—for the most part—and insurance companies denied the existence of the practice, but the evidence to the contrary was overwhelming."[40]

The Fair Housing Act

By the mid-1960s housing discrimination was rampant throughout the United States. President Lyndon B. Johnson, who was known for being a civil rights champion, was candid and outspoken about wanting Congress to pass fair housing legislation. Organizations such as the National Association for the Advancement of Colored People (NAACP) and the National Committee Against Discrimination in Housing lobbied heavily for the govern-

President Lyndon B. Johnson (right) meets with Martin Luther King Jr. (left) in the Oval Office of the White House in 1963. Johnson was a civil rights champion who pushed Congress to pass fair housing legislation.

ment to pass such legislation. Finally, their efforts paid off. After a fierce debate in both houses of Congress, the Fair Housing Act was passed on April 10, 1968. The following day, Johnson signed it into law, saying, "I do not exaggerate when I say that the proudest moments of my Presidency have been times such as this when I have signed into law the promises of a century."[41] Johnson went on to say that the legislation was a fitting tribute to Martin Luther King Jr., who had been assassinated the week before.

> **"Mortgage lenders literally drew red lines around minority areas and instructed loan officers to deny any mortgage applications inside the areas so marked."[40]**
>
> —Dean Browning Webb, an attorney from Vancouver, Washington

The Fair Housing Act expanded on the Civil Rights Act of 1964. It banned people from refusing to rent or sell to anyone solely based on race. It outlawed racial discrimination in real estate terms and conditions, as well as in advertising. Real estate agents were prohibited from commenting about the race of neighbors or potential property buyers in order to promote panic selling. In essence, says Massey, the Fair Housing Act "expressly banned many of the public actions and private practices that had evolved over the years to deny blacks access to housing."[42]

A Segregated Society

As important and historic as the Fair Housing Act was, it could not magically cure America's housing discrimination problem. The law was intended to prohibit future discrimination, but it could not erase the damage that was done in the past. The problem of housing segregation was too deeply entrenched in American society. By the time the legislation was enacted, says Economic Policy Institute researcher Richard Rothstein, "the patterns of segregation had been firmly established. Simply passing a Fair Housing Act did not enable African-Americans who were previously living in urban areas to relocate to the suburbs from which they'd been excluded."[43]

Despite passage of the Fair Housing Act, housing remained segregated throughout the United States. Although it was now illegal to discriminate when selling or renting property, no law could force white people and black people to live in the same neighborhoods. By 1980 the African American population in America's cities had more than doubled from 6.1 million in 1950 to 15.3 million. Also by this time, white Americans had begun steadily moving away from the inner cities and into the surrounding suburbs. This movement came to be known as "white flight." Those who remained in the inner cities were, for the most part, low-income African Americans.

> **"It doesn't take much to stir people to white flight; they feared black people."[44]**
>
> —Ira Harris, a retired lawyer from Detroit, Michigan

One city whose population changed dramatically in the early to mid-twentieth century was Detroit, Michigan. In 1930 the city's population was slightly over 92 percent white. By 1980 the white population had plummeted to less than 34 percent. "It doesn't take much to stir people to white flight; they feared black people,"[44] says retired lawyer Ira Harris, who grew up in Detroit and lived there until the 1980s.

Upholding the Law

Today a number of agencies and organizations closely monitor housing discrimination in the United States. Since 1988 the government agency called the US Department of Housing and Urban Development (HUD) has been charged with enforcing the Fair Housing Act. One of its primary responsibilities is to investigate complaints of housing discrimination. Also formed in 1988 is the National Fair Housing Alliance (NFHA), which is a consortium of civil rights and fair housing groups and individuals. In tandem with HUD, the NFHA investigates suspect policies and practices and then prepares reports of its findings.

In its April 2017 fair housing trends report, the NFHA makes it clear that housing segregation is not a thing of the past. "Every major metropolitan area in the United States is heavily segregated

Discrimination Is Harmful to Health

Dealing with any kind of discrimination can be both frustrating and upsetting. Housing discrimination, in particular, can have lasting effects on a person's health. An October 2017 joint survey by the Harvard T.H. Chan School of Public Health, National Public Radio, and the Robert Wood Johnson Foundation examined the prevalence and effects of discrimination. The researchers concluded that those who are subjected to discrimination have a higher incidence of health problems and a lower life expectancy than people who are not affected by it. "A safe, decent, affordable [residence] can act like a vaccine," says Megan Sandel, a physician and researcher at Boston Medical Center. "It can keep you healthy now and in the future."

Quoted in Emily Sullivan, "Looking for a Home When Your Name Is Hispanic and Finding Discrimination Instead," NPR, November 2, 2017. www.npr.org.

by race and ethnicity," the report authors write. Referring to practices such as racially restrictive covenants, real estate discrimination, and redlining, the authors state, "Contemporary versions of the same practices continue to this day."[45] As a result of continued segregation, says the NFHA, approximately half of all black people and 40 percent of Latinos live in neighborhoods with no presence of white people. And the average white person lives in a neighborhood that is nearly 80 percent white.

The report reveals that during 2016 there were 28,181 housing discrimination complaints. Yet that is believed to be only a fraction of the actual offenses, since most people do not report racial or ethnic discrimination. The NFHA estimates that at least 4 million cases of housing discrimination occur every year. Nearly all the reported cases involve rental transactions. The owner of a Florida mobile home park, for instance, was cited for discriminating against African Americans. When they inquired about mobile homes or available lots in the park, the owner said that none were available. If white potential renters contacted him, they were told that homes and lots were available.

The NFHA report also revealed that some banks are still engaging in the illegal practice of redlining. One of the cases cited in the report involved Hudson City Savings Bank, which is headquartered in Paramus, New Jersey. The report states that the bank intentionally avoided doing mortgage business with blacks and Latinos between 2009 and 2013. The report also cited Associated Bank of Green Bay, Wisconsin, for denying mortgage loans to black and Latino applicants from 2008 to 2010. According to the report authors, these sorts of cases "highlight the persistence and variability of housing discrimination in this nation."[46]

Trouble for Facebook

Investigations have also found that housing discrimination is fostered by Internet activity. Social media sites like Facebook make it possible for ads to be viewed only by certain groups and not by others. In other words, seller or rental agents can place ads on Facebook that intentionally exclude blacks and Latinos or other minority groups—and they have been doing exactly that, according to the nonprofit news organization ProPublica.

> **"Imagine if, during the Jim Crow era, a newspaper offered advertisers the option of placing ads only in copies that went to white readers. That's basically what Facebook is doing nowadays."[47]**
>
> —Julia Angwin and Terry Parris Jr., reporters for ProPublica

In October 2016 ProPublica investigated Facebook's advertising options. The group found that along with targeting users based on their interests, advertisers had the ability to single people out by race, gender, or other sensitive factors. ProPublica reporters Julia Angwin and Terry Parris Jr. explain, "Imagine if, during the Jim Crow era, a newspaper offered advertisers the option of placing ads only in copies that went to white readers. That's basically what Facebook is doing nowadays."[47] This sort of exclusionary advertising is in violation of federal law.

At the time of ProPublica's investigation, Facebook's advertising portal, where businesses can create ads, offered the option to "narrow audience." Upon clicking that, ad creators could exclude African Americans, Asian Americans, and/or four categories of

Hispanics. There was no similar option for excluding white audiences. ProPublica created a test ad through the portal, targeting Facebook users who were house hunting. The ad excluded all minority audiences—meaning that if people were interested in buying or renting a house, they would only be able to see this ad if they were white. Upon seeing the ad that ProPublica was able to place, civil rights attorney John Relman was horrified. "This is massively illegal," he says. "This is about as blatant a violation of the federal Fair Housing Act as one can find."[48]

On November 7, 2016, three people who had used Facebook to find housing sued the company for violating federal antidiscrimination laws. Facebook officials denied that any rules or laws had been broken but vowed to do a major overhaul of their system to crack down on discriminatory advertising. That did not happen quite as the company stated, however. In November 2017 ProPublica was again able to create dozens of discriminatory ads through the Facebook portal. "Under its own policies, Facebook should have flagged these ads, and prevented the posting of some of them," says ProPublica reporters. "Its failure to do so revives questions about whether the company is in compliance with federal fair housing rules, as well as about its ability and commitment to police discriminatory advertising on the world's largest social network."[49]

A Problem That Needs Solving

When President Lyndon B. Johnson proudly signed into law the Fair Housing Act, he truly believed that it would make a world of difference for people of color who had been discriminated against when trying to find a place to live. And in many ways the law has helped. Today, for instance, dishonest practices such as redlining and panic peddling, as well as deliberate refusal to sell or rent to people of color, are illegal, and people who engage in them can be slapped with huge fines. Yet as research and anecdotal evidence have consistently shown, housing discrimination remains a serious and persistent problem.

CHAPTER 4

Employment and Education

Many Americans believe that racial discrimination is much less of a problem than it once was. And in many ways it is. More black teens are graduating from high school. More of them go on to earn associate's or bachelor's degrees. And as of December 2017, unemployment among African Americans is at an all-time low of 6.8 percent, compared with 16 percent in December 2009. Still, African Americans and other people of color are way behind white Americans in the number who graduate from college, are able to find good jobs, and are paid fairly for their work.

Discriminatory Hiring

Researchers who study economic and social equality cite various reasons for this inequality. Among the reasons they give is racial discrimination. Lincoln Quillian, a sociology professor at Northwestern University, explains, "It is often suggested that prejudice and discrimination are fading out over time. . . . But we found striking stability in discrimination against African-Americans."[50] Quillian is referring to a study that he conducted along with researchers from Harvard University and the Institute of Social Research in Oslo, Norway. The focus of their study was to investigate incidents of job hiring discrimination—and they found a high prevalence of it.

Quillian's group analyzed results from many different studies conducted over a twenty-five year period from 1990 to 2015. They found that during those years, 55,842 job applications were submitted for 26,326 positions in a variety of fields. The researchers uncovered some compelling evidence of racial discrimination in hiring practices. They found that white applicants consistently received an average of 36 percent more callbacks for job interviews than did African American applicants who were equally qualified. Faring only slightly better were Latinos, who received 24 percent fewer callbacks than did white applicants with the same qualifications. These findings were troubling to the researchers. Although discrimination may have diminished over the years, in job hiring they saw no improvement over the twenty-five years of the study. The report authors write, "African Americans remain substantially disadvantaged relative to equally qualified whites, and we see little indication of progress over time."[51]

The Law Is Clear but Not Always Obeyed

Employment-related discrimination, including racial discrimination, is illegal. It is prohibited under a federal law known as Title VII, which is part of the Civil Rights Act of 1964. Title VII applies to all entities that employ fifteen or more individuals, including private employers; government employers (federal, state, and local); and private and public colleges and universities. A federal agency known as the Equal Employment Opportunity Commission (EEOC) is responsible for enforcing Title VII and taking legal action when the law is violated.

Under Title VII, an employer is not allowed to discriminate against anyone based on race, color, religion, sex, or national origin. Title VII forbids discrimination in any aspect of employment, from advertising job opportunities to hiring and promotions to firing and layoffs. When a job opening is posted, for example, employers may not state, insinuate, or suggest that people of certain races are preferred over others. When someone has been hired, race cannot be used to deny compensation or benefits or be used as a basis for promotions or layoffs.

Despite the law being clear on what employment practices are forbidden, employers do not always abide by the law. Research

A woman interviews with a potential employer. Research has found that white applicants receive 36 percent more job callbacks than African American applicants.

has shown that people of color are regularly discriminated against in businesses and corporations nationwide. "Even among well-intended employers, racial bias may lurk in hiring decisions," Quillian and his study coauthors write. "Whether conscious or not, bias continues to affect decision making."[52]

During an October 2017 joint survey by Harvard T.H. Chan School of Public Health, National Public Radio, and the Robert Wood Johnson Foundation, participants were asked questions about their personal experiences with discrimination. When asked if they had ever felt discriminated against when applying for jobs, 56 percent of African Americans, 33 percent of Latinos, and 27 percent of Asian Americans said they had. In addition, 57 percent of African Americans, 32 percent of Latinos, and 25 percent of Asian Americans said they had been discriminated against in terms of equal pay or being promoted at work.

Discrimination Does Not Pay

One company that was sued by the EEOC for hiring discrimination is Bass Pro Outdoor World, a retailer of hunting, fishing, and camping merchandise. Discriminatory incidents reportedly occurred at numerous Bass Pro stores throughout the United States. "One of the most shocking aspects of this case was its scope," says R. Scott Oswald, an attorney with a Washington, DC, employment law group. "The EEOC alleged a pattern of racist hiring that had infected literally dozens of Bass Pro locations across the United States."[53]

One Bass Pro store that was cited in the lawsuit was located in Katy, Texas, a city in the Houston area. The general manager complained to the human resources manager about the racial makeup of the store's employees. "You need to hire some white people," the general manager said, remarking that it was "getting a little dark in here."[54]

> **"The EEOC alleged a pattern of racist hiring that had infected literally dozens of Bass Pro locations across the United States."[53]**
>
> —R. Scott Oswald, an attorney with a Washington, DC, employment law group

In a Bass Pro store in Louisiana, according to the EEOC lawsuit, a human resources manager asked the store manager why a qualified black job applicant was rejected. The manager answered that the young man did not fit the company profile. When pressed for more information, the manager reportedly said, "We don't hire niggers."[55]

The EEOC lawsuit listed other incidents at stores in other states. In Indiana, the lawsuit stated, a store manager discarded job applications if an applicant's name sounded like a black person's name. At another Indiana store, the lawsuit stated, someone in security was heard saying that Hispanic people "should be shot at the border by the border patrol."[56] A similar racial slur about Hispanic applicants was reportedly made by the general manager of a store in Broken Arrow, Oklahoma. In Peal, Mississippi, a Bass Pro human resources manager testified in court that corporate executives were dedicated to hiring only white people to work at the stores.

In July 2017 Bass Pro Outdoor World agreed to pay $10.5 million to settle the lawsuit. Although the company did not admit to violating any laws, company officials stressed their commitment to hiring a more diverse workforce. They agreed to take steps to ensure fairer and more equal hiring practices at their stores throughout the country.

Racial Harassment

Employers also have a responsibility to ensure that their employees are not harassed while on the job. Legally, harassment falls under the category of discrimination, which means it is prohibited under the Title VII law. The EEOC defines harassment as "unwelcome conduct" based on race, color, religion, sex, national origin, disability, or other factors. Harassers might include supervisors, coworkers, or nonemployees, and a wide variety of actions can constitute harassment: offensive jokes, racial slurs, name-calling, ridicule or mockery, insults or put-downs, the display of offensive objects or pictures, or physical threats and/or assaults. The EEOC emphasizes that harassment is not the same as "petty slights, annoyances," or minor isolated incidents. Rather, the EEOC says, the offenses must create a work environment "that would be intimidating, hostile, or offensive to reasonable people."[57]

"It's just these little daily aggressions that really add up over time. Having a lack of people who look like you in general is demoralizing."[59]

—Qichen Zhang, a former employee at Google

Qichen Zhang endured such relentless harassment when she worked for Google that she ended up quitting her job. Zhang, who graduated from Harvard University, was hired in 2013 as a technical specialist. Initially, she was thrilled; Google was known for being a progressive and highly desirable employer. "Everybody wants to work at Google,"[58] she says. It was not long after starting her job, however, that she discovered a very different work environment than what she had envisioned. Most of her coworkers were white males, and she could not keep from feeling out of place, and even unwelcome.

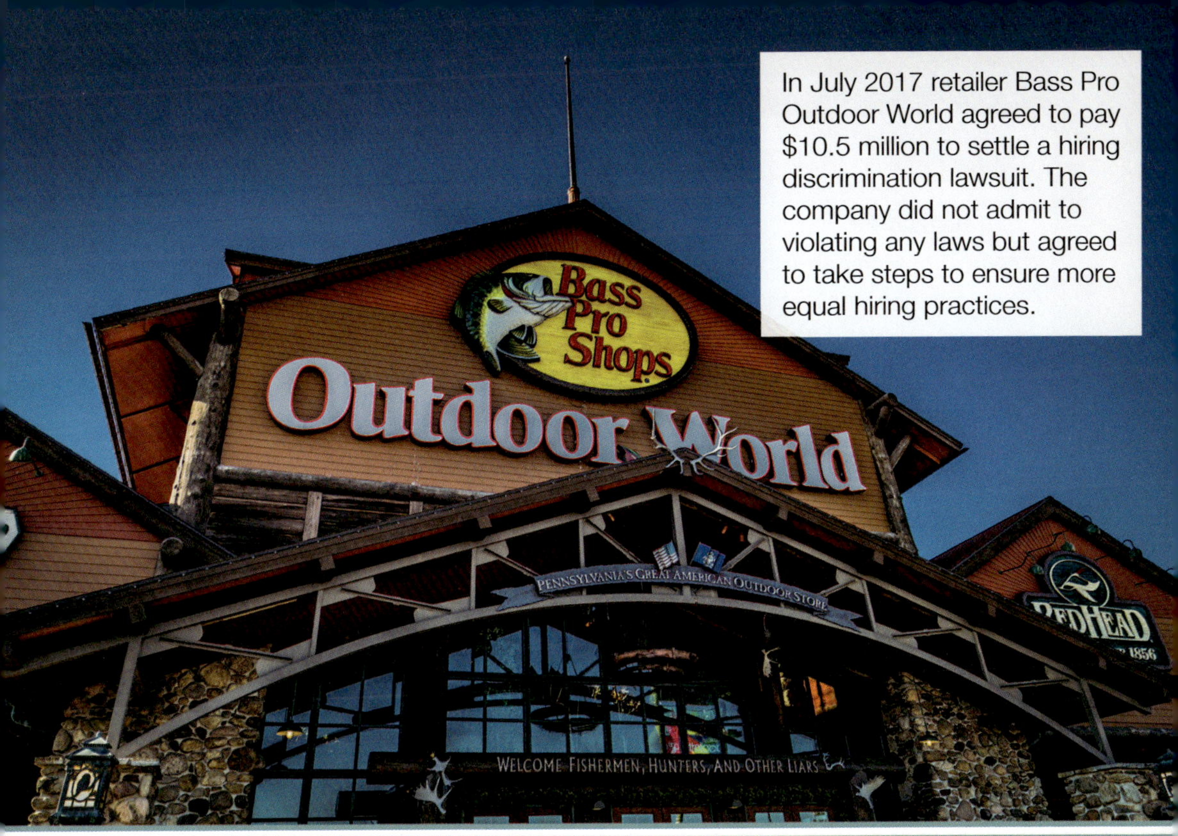

In July 2017 retailer Bass Pro Outdoor World agreed to pay $10.5 million to settle a hiring discrimination lawsuit. The company did not admit to violating any laws but agreed to take steps to ensure more equal hiring practices.

"It's just these little daily aggressions that really add up over time," says Zhang. "Having a lack of people who look like you in general is demoralizing."[59]

One incident was particularly upsetting to Zhang. She was in the middle of the office when a white male colleague started making crass jokes about her hiring. Zhang explains, "He said, 'It must've been really easy for you to get your job because you're an Asian woman and people assume you're good at math.' It was absolutely stunning. I remember me just emotionally shutting down."[60] A few months later, convinced that she had no future at Google, Zhang resigned.

Another employee who worked at Google as a technical specialist, a young black woman who wishes to remain anonymous, says she encountered prejudice and discrimination on a daily basis. "I felt like I didn't belong nor did anybody want me to belong,"[61] she says. She was the only black woman on her team, and she says that while walking throughout the Google campus, employees would frequently ask to see her identification. She

Résumé Whitening

Job hunting can be stressful for anyone. People searching for jobs face tough competition and an economy in which high-paying positions are in short supply. Nonwhite job applicants face these barriers along with another that is especially daunting: racial discrimination. Studies have shown that compared with white applicants, people of color get far fewer interviews—even if their qualifications are the same or better. Researchers who study this issue say people are being screened out based on racial clues found on their résumés, which is illegal. With that in mind, minority job hunters have begun "whitening" their résumés by deleting references to their race.

Asian Americans, for instance, have Americanized names on their résumés, such as replacing Lei with Luke. African Americans have omitted mentions of race by not including black organizations to which they belong or purposely listed outdoor hobbies that are popular among whites, such as kayaking or hiking. These tactics have proved to be effective. According to a 2016 study, 25 percent of black job candidates received callbacks after whitening their résumés, compared with 10 percent who left their ethnic details intact. Of Asian Americans, 21 percent were called for interviews if they whitened their résumés, compared with 11.5 percent whose résumés contained racial clues. Many minority job hunters have put this technique to use, but not everyone is willing to do that. "I wouldn't consider whitening my résumé," said one college student, "because if they don't accept my racial identity, I don't see how I would fit in that job."

Quoted in Dina Gerdeman, "Minorities Who 'Whiten' Resumes Get More Job Interviews," *Forbes*, May 17, 2017. www.forbes.com.

observed that nonblack employees were rarely asked for their IDs. She often heard people telling racist jokes and was left out of social events and even group e-mails. Being treated differently because of her race was terribly upsetting and started to affect her mental health. "There were times I cried at my desk," she says. Finally, after working at Google for two years, she quit her job. "I was invisible," she says. "It was like I didn't matter. So what was the point of being there?"[62]

In Pursuit of Fairness and Equality

Although people may not agree about the severity of racial discrimination in employment, there is convincing evidence that it exists. Through the years, civil rights advocates have proposed and supported numerous efforts to help people of color have a fair and equal chance in the workplace. One of these efforts dates back to 1961. That year President John F. Kennedy issued an executive order in which he stated that discrimination because of race, creed, color, or national origin was contrary to the principles and policies of the US Constitution. He then proceeded to describe what he expected to happen in order to eliminate and prevent discrimination.

President John F. Kennedy was a dedicated proponent of fair hiring practices. He established the President's Committee on Equal Employment Opportunity.

Kennedy established the President's Committee on Equal Employment Opportunity, which a few years later became the EEOC. He mandated that there be no employment discrimination in government agencies nor among contracted individuals or agencies. Kennedy's intention was to emphasize the government's firm commitment to equal opportunities for everyone, without regard to race or other factors. In his executive order, he referred to "affirmative action," and that term came to represent any effort that was intended to level the playing field for minorities.

> **"This is the next and the more profound stage of the battle for civil rights. We seek not just freedom but opportunity."[63]**
>
> —Lyndon B. Johnson, the thirty-sixth president of the United States

After Kennedy's death in 1963, Vice President Lyndon B. Johnson assumed the presidency. Like his predecessor, he was passionate about equal opportunity, and he continued the work that Kennedy had started. Johnson believed strongly in affirmative action and touted the importance of policies that helped people of color achieve equality. In June 1965 he gave the commencement address at Howard University, a historically black college in Washington, DC. "Freedom is not enough," said Johnson.

> You do not wipe away the scars of centuries by saying: "Now you are free to go where you want, and do as you desire, and choose the leaders you please." You do not take a person who, for years, has been hobbled by chains and liberate him, bring him up to the starting line of a race and then say, "You are free to compete with all the others," and still justly believe that you have been completely fair. Thus it is not enough just to open the gates of opportunity. All our citizens must have the ability to walk through those gates. This is the next and the more profound stage of the battle for civil rights. We seek not just freedom but opportunity.[63]

Growth of Affirmative Action

Over the following years, businesses and corporations nationwide developed affirmative action programs and put them into practice. These programs included a concerted effort to recruit minorities to apply for jobs and, in the process, to increase diversity in the workplace. Progress did not happen overnight, but hiring practices and employment policies gradually became less discriminatory than they had been. Colleges and universities also adopted affirmative action admission policies, which were intended to provide equal access to groups (such as minorities) that had historically been excluded or underrepresented. These policies led to a steady increase in enrollment rates for African American and Latino students.

A Woman, a Scientist, a Pioneer

In the early 1900s racial discrimination was extraordinarily common, including in places of employment. The opportunities for people of color were slim; in fact, many dropped out of school by the eighth grade. For Katherine Coleman Johnson, however, race was never a barrier. Born in a small West Virginia town in 1918, Johnson was taught that she was equal to anyone, regardless of skin color. It was obvious from a very young age that she was highly intelligent. She was fascinated by numbers and excelled in math. She started high school at age ten and graduated at age fourteen. She earned a college degree by the time she reached eighteen.

In 1953, after years of teaching, Johnson went to work at the agency that is now the National Aeronautics and Space Administration (NASA). This was before electronic computers, and people like Johnson with superior math skills were called "computers." She was a computer, she says, "when the computer wore a skirt." She worked on NASA's space programs and was the first to calculate the distance between the earth and the moon. For astronaut Alan Shepard, the first American in space, Johnson was the person who calculated the trajectory (route) of his spacecraft. She was hand-picked by astronaut John Glenn to do the calculations for *Friendship 7*, the first mission to orbit Earth. She continued to work at NASA until 1986, and in November 2015, President Barack Obama presented her with the Presidential Medal of Freedom.

Quoted in Jim Hodges, "She Was a Computer When Computers Wore Skirts," NASA, August 7, 2017. www.nasa.gov.

One affirmative action success story is Ronald W. Johnson. As a young man, Johnson, who is African American, moved to California from his native Brooklyn, New York. Now the director of financial aid at the University of California–Los Angeles (UCLA), Johnson shares his thoughts about what affirmative action did for him:

> I know for certain that were it not for affirmative action, many doors would have been closed. My accomplishments weren't given to me because of who I knew, or who my father knew. They weren't handed to me because of how well I played sports. I earned my accomplishments through hard work, integrity and intelligence. But I knew I had a lot to be thankful for, most of which were the many doors of opportunity that opened for me to show my attributes.[64]

Johnson cannot help but think about what might have happened if he had not been given the opportunities that helped him get to where he is today. "My future, and the future of those lives I have touched, would never be realized," he says. "Whether it's due to racism, closed doors, or perhaps the non-existence of affirmative action, the results would have been the same—lack of opportunity."[65]

Another person who benefited from affirmative action is Supreme Court justice Sonia Sotomayor. Sotomayor, whose parents are from Puerto Rico, is the high court's first Hispanic justice. After her father's death, Sotomayor was raised by her mother in the Bronx borough of New York City. Thanks to affirmative action policies at Princeton University and Yale Law School, along with scholarship funds, she received a superb education at two of the top schools in the United States. "For me," says Sotomayor, "[affirmative action] was a door-opener that changed the course of my life."[66]

The Backlash

Affirmative action has opened doors and provided much-needed assistance to young people of color. But support for the program has steadily declined over the years. One of the strongest objections is that affirmative action has led to "reverse discrimination," in which qualified white applicants are passed over in favor of minority applicants. "You can't be a minority in this society without having someone express disapproval about affirmative action,"[67] says Sotomayor.

The most contentious debate over affirmative action is related to education. Many people believe that colleges and universities should not use race as a factor when choosing students to be admitted. That belief is what led a young white woman named Abigail Fisher to sue the University of Texas after she was denied admission. Fisher claimed racial discrimination because the school used race as one of many factors in its admissions process. When lower courts ruled against her, she petitioned to go before the US Supreme Court, and her request was granted. In 2014, in a 4–3 decision, the justices ruled that the University of Texas's use of race as an admissions criterion was constitutional.

That same year the Supreme Court handed affirmative action opponents a victory as well. In a case that upheld Michigan's ban on affirmative action, the justices essentially paved the way for states to allow or disallow the program. To date, eight states—Arizona, California, Florida, Michigan, Nebraska, New Hampshire, Oklahoma, and Washington—have banned the use of race in college admissions. As time goes by, legal experts predict more legal challenges and court rulings on affirmative action.

Many Unknowns

Nobody knows what will happen with affirmative action in the future—whether it will get stronger or be ruled unconstitutional and disappear from policy manuals altogether. Nor does anyone know what will happen with racial discrimination, which research has shown is not only prevalent but a serious problem in hiring and employment practices. For people of color, who experience racial discrimination on a daily basis, the day when these problems disappear cannot come soon enough.

CHAPTER 5

Efforts to End Racial Discrimination

Throughout the United States, civil rights groups, individuals, and local governments are taking steps to level the playing field for minorities and help eliminate racial discrimination. But according to those who are still being discriminated against, the problem is far from solved. One example is the breakdown in relationships between police and African American citizens. Black people in many cities are convinced that police single them out and harass them, which creates a volatile and potentially dangerous situation. When efforts are made to strengthen and build these relationships, communities and the people who live in them benefit immensely.

The close friendship between Rob Dance and Shaun Corbett is living proof of how beneficial such relationship building can be. Their friendship is often called unlikely because of how vastly different their backgrounds and lives are. Dance, who lives in Charlotte, North Carolina, is a white police captain. Corbett, also from Charlotte, is a black barber who once hated all police. He has a long criminal record, including time spent in prison for drugs and other offenses. But neither of the men cares about their differences. "Rob's my guy," says Corbett. "Like, he's really my guy."[68]

Cops and Barbers

The first time Dance walked into Corbett's barber shop in Charlotte, everything seemed to stop. There was dead silence. Dance said hello, but as he gazed at all the black faces staring back at him, he knew without a doubt that he was an object of suspicion. People instinctively wondered what sort of problem had brought him to their neighborhood and what he wanted from them. Then Dance walked over to Corbett, and the two men hugged and greeted each other. As soon as people saw that, they relaxed. "Slowly they realized that everything was gonna be okay,"[69] says Dance.

Along with being friends, Dance and Corbett are partners in Cops and Barbers, a program that builds relationships between police officers and young black males in their city. Corbett started the program in 2014 a short time after Michael Brown was shot and killed by a white police officer in Ferguson, Missouri. After a life of crime, Corbett had worked hard to turn his life around. He was distraught over Brown's death, as well as the disturbingly high number of other young African American males who had suffered the same fate. He feared for the lives of his own two sons, especially his oldest, who was a teenager and driving his own car.

Corbett had taught his boys everything he believed a father should teach his sons. He taught them to be kind, considerate, courteous, and law abiding. But he also knew that young black men had been shot and killed by police officers even when they were unarmed and doing nothing wrong—and this terrified him. In 2010, after he bought his barber shop, Corbett began hosting informal get-togethers. He invited people young and old to his shop to talk about racial issues and relationships with police. Corbett knew that the group could be a lot more effective if it involved police officers, and that is what gave him the idea for Cops and Barbers.

Corbett believed that his sons and other young black men needed positive exposure to police officers. They needed to see police as something other than a threat. He was also convinced that police could benefit from developing relationships with people in their communities. If they really got to know the people they served, Corbett thought, it could change behavior on both sides. "I have yet to see an officer shoot someone that they know or they've had positive encounters with," he says. "I am 100 percent certain that if I get pulled over by Rob, he's not going to shoot me in the street."[70]

Since Corbett and Dance have been working together, their friendship has grown stronger. So has their commitment to Cops and Barbers. They and others in the group visit schools to talk about race-related issues and to tutor kids who need help in school. They host special events like pizza dinners, turkey drives at Thanksgiving, and book drives. They pair up police officers

Throughout the United States, groups, individuals, and local governments are taking steps to eliminate racial discrimination. Black people in many cities feel that police single them out and harass them.

and young men from the neighborhood, who go out to dinner together. This is awkward for everyone at first, as Corbett explains: "It's actually funny because everybody's sitting there stone-faced. Nobody's saying a word."[71] But by the time the food is served, says Corbett, they are all talking about their favorite sports teams and players, and everyone is having a good time.

> **"I have yet to see an officer shoot someone that they know or they've had positive encounters with."[70]**
>
> —Shaun Corbett, a black man from Charlotte, North Carolina, who founded Cops and Barbers

There have also been some tough times, though. In 2016, after the shooting death of a black man from Charlotte named Keith Lamont Scott, a team of prosecutors opted not to charge the police officer who shot him. Protestors took to the streets, shouting, demanding justice, and accusing police of getting away with murder. Dance was there with the police, and Corbett was there with the protestors, and they both did what they could to help ease tensions in the city. After that, someone asked Corbett if he thought Cops and Barbers was a failure because of what happened to Scott. He answered with an emphatic "No," adding: "Think about how many situations probably didn't happen because these officers are now knowing people in the community. Just think about how many situations could have . . . been prevented that we don't even know [about]."[72]

Both Corbett and Dance are aware that they cannot fix everything that is broken between law enforcement and the communities they serve. But they are convinced Cops and Barbers is a start, and an important one. "Me and Rob, we're not going to end all this," says Corbett, adding that people need to do their part in helping their communities. "Because, you know, war is won over a series of small battles."[73]

An Issue of Trust

To improve relations between police officers and the public, many people in communities with large black populations have expressed a willingness to partner with law enforcement. Although African

Americans often fear rather than trust the police, many respect the law and understand that police officers are charged with upholding it. This was revealed during a 2017 Urban Institute study titled "How Do People in High-Crime, Low-Income Communities View the Police?" Yet even as respondents expressed positive feelings about law enforcement, they were also wary of how they would be treated by police. "Many people from these same communities don't believe that police are fair or just in how they apply the law, particularly when it comes to African Americans,"[74] says a February 2017 article about the study.

> **"Quite simply, reductions in violent crime are not possible without meaningful representation of—and engagement with—the residents most affected by it."[75]**
>
> —Nancy La Vigne, Jocelyn Fontaine, and Anamika Dwivedi, who are with the Urban Institute

Nearly thirteen hundred people participated in the Urban Institute study, the majority of whom were African American. They reside in poor, high-crime neighborhoods in six US cities: Birmingham, Alabama; Fort Worth, Texas; Gary, Indiana; Minneapolis, Minnesota; Pittsburgh, Pennsylvania; and Stockton, California.

The residents' overall distrust of law enforcement was apparent in how they answered questions about policing. For instance, only 30 percent of residents believe that police in their communities respect people's rights, give people a chance to tell their side of the story before deciding what to do, and treat people with dignity and respect. Only slightly more than that (33 percent) think that police explain their decisions and actions so people can understand, and 34 percent think police try to help people they deal with. The study authors write, "Quite simply, reductions in violent crime are not possible without meaningful representation of—and engagement with—the residents most affected by it."[75]

Communities Taking Action

Police departments throughout the United States have implemented programs and practices that help strengthen relation-

Blacks and Whites Differ on How to Achieve Racial Equality

Black and white Americans do not see eye to eye when it comes to some of the specifics of how blacks can achieve racial quality, according to a 2016 Pew Research Center poll. While many in both groups value working together to solve problems, blacks are much more supportive than whites of other strategies such as getting more blacks elected to public office and organizing protests and rallies.

Percent saying _____ would be a very effective tactic for groups that work to help blacks achieve equality

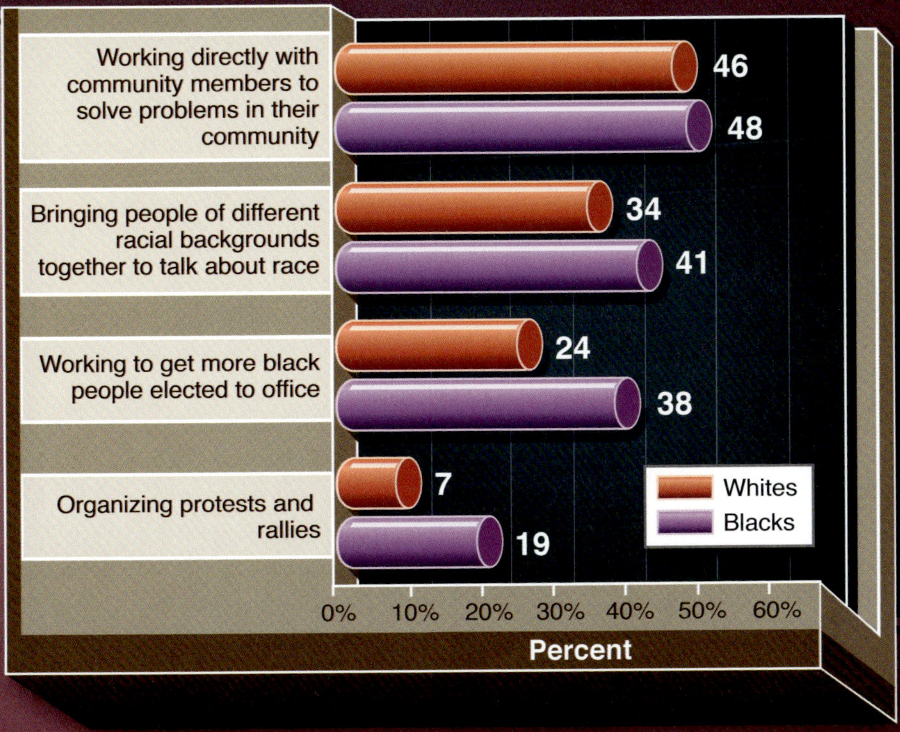

Source: Pew Research Center, "On Views of Race and Inequality, Blacks and Whites Are Worlds Apart," June 27, 2016. www.pewsocialtrends.org.

ships between officers and the communities they serve. One city that has been lauded for its efforts is Charleston, West Virginia, a city of just over fifty thousand people. In October 2015 faith leaders, representatives of local organizations, and law enforcement personnel came together to address racial disparities in arrests by the Charleston Police Department. According to the department's own data, the arrest rate for black people was more than double that for whites, and this was a problem that needed action.

At that first meeting, participants had a lengthy, candid discussion with the city's police chief. After sharing concerns and fears for the community, the group members developed an action plan. They began working together to address racial disparities in policing procedures and are seeing positive results from their efforts. "West Virginia hasn't historically been on the forefront in addressing racial and economic inequality," says economic justice advocate Lida Shepherd, "but I'm proud to say that for once, we might be leading the pack."[76]

> **"West Virginia hasn't historically been on the forefront in addressing racial and economic inequality, but I'm proud to say that for once, we might be leading the pack."[76]**
>
> —Lida Shepherd, an economic justice advocate from Charleston, West Virginia

Another city that has made great strides in improving relationships between the African American community and police officers is Minneapolis, Minnesota. In August 2016 the Minneapolis Police Department enacted some major changes, such as requiring that police officers participate in de-escalation training. This involves training officers to exhaust all reasonable means of defusing potentially violent situations before resorting to force. Officers are also trained to recognize factors that could potentially contribute to someone's lack of compliance with the law. These could include anything from language barriers and/or drug use to a mental health crisis. And in a case where force becomes necessary, officers are encouraged to first announce their intent to use force. On behalf of officers' emotional well-being, the department put measures in place to better identify troubled officers so they can get the help they need.

One of the most significant changes to the Minneapolis Police Department came about in 2017. For the first time in the city's

The Friendly Neighborhood Police Officer

Like many cities, Detroit, Michigan, has struggled with African American residents feeling distrustful of police. One way Detroit officials are trying to rebuild trust is through a neighborhood police program, which helps police officers develop ties to the communities they serve. Baron Coleman is one of the neighborhood officers. He gives his cell phone number to all residents who live in his precinct, and he encourages them to call for any reason. "When you call 911, officers are coming to an emergency," says Coleman. "They get in, catch the bad guy and go. But with a neighborhood police officer, they might call me about anything from a barking dog, to a basketball rim in the street, not liking the neighbor, neighbor not liking them, people parking on their grass."

When the only interactions people have with police are during conflicts or criminal activities, says Coleman, these interactions are typically negative. But, he says, "if I come by your street every day, wave at you, be nice to you, be nice to your family," people will start to develop trust. One look inside the trunk of Coleman's police car offers a glimpse at the relationships he has developed with residents. It contains camping chairs, so he can hang out at a park if there is a neighborhood gathering or a game; a crate of juice boxes for the kids; and even oven mitts, so he can help grill at neighborhood cookouts. For Coleman, being prepared for happy events as well as problems is an important part of his job.

Quoted in Jennifer Guerra, "How to Improve Community-Police Relations? Here Are Two Approaches," Michigan Radio State of Opportunity, August 17, 2016. http://stateofopportunity.michiganradio.org.

150-year history, the department is being led by an African American police chief. The new chief, Medaria Arradondo, has been in law enforcement for thirty years and is well aware of the divide between black communities and the police officers that serve them. He passionately wants that to change in Minneapolis, where he grew up. "We know there have been incidents that have occurred in our city and across our country that have shaken the foundation of trust between our communities and our police department,"

In 2017 the Minneapolis Police Department appointed its first African American police chief. The new chief, Medaria Arradondo, intends to improve the relationship between police and the black communities they serve.

says Arradondo. "And so I'm committed that when the last chapter is written, the Minneapolis Police Department will be on the right side of history."[77]

A Partnership Approach

Programs that strengthen relationships between law enforcement and black citizens are a high priority for many communities because when those relationships break down, people's lives are at risk. But other aspects of racial discrimination must also be addressed, although people do not always agree on how to go about doing that. Some antidiscrimination efforts have been successful due to businesses and civil rights groups working together. One example is a partnership between the NAACP and Airbnb, an online service that enables people to lease or rent short-term lodging.

This partnership came about because Airbnb's reputation was at stake. The company has been accused of blatant discrimination on more than one occasion. In one instance, a host refused to rent her mountain cabin when she found out the renter, Dyne Suh, was Asian American. Suh and some friends had rented the cabin so they could spend a weekend skiing. Minutes before they arrived, she received a text message from the host that stated, "I wouldn't rent it to u if u were the last person on earth" and "One word says it all. Asian."[78] The host was charged with discrimination and required to pay a $5,000 fine.

Airbnb's discriminatory practices were investigated by researcher Dennis Zhang. He sent out hundreds of housing requests to Airbnb hosts in Chicago, Illinois; Seattle, Washington; and Boston, Massachusetts. The requests were identical, except for the names of the fictitious guests. On some, Zhang used stereotypically black names such as Laquisha or Jamal, and on others he used stereotypically white names like Emily or Greg. What he found was that the applications with black-sounding names were 18 percent less likely to be accepted than the distinctly white names. This was in line with what people of color had reported when they had tried to rent or lease from Airbnb hosts.

This blatant discrimination is against Airbnb's rules for hosts. But it is challenging for the company to enforce its rule of fair and equal treatment of customers because Airbnb does not own the properties that people rent. Rather, it merely facilitates connections between owners and potential renters. By partnering with the NAACP, Airbnb will make a concerted effort to recruit more minority hosts, as well as to target communities of color in property promotions. In addition, Airbnb has embarked on a plan to diversify its workforce, and the NAACP will assist with this.

Stealth Approach to Diversifying

The future of affirmative action is uncertain, and eight US states have already banned the practice. Yet colleges and universities want to attract a diverse student body, so they are seeking creative approaches in doing so. One of these schools is UCLA. Because California is among the states that prohibits the use of race in college admissions, UCLA has embarked on an aggressive new effort to boost its minority student population without violating the law. "I call it intrusive recruiting," says Youlonda Copeland-Morgan, who leads UCLA's student recruitment program. "We're in your face. We're out there like college coaches."

Copeland-Morgan, who is black, supervises a team of recruiting professionals who work with schools and churches throughout Los Angeles. They identify the best and brightest minority kids, like Damion Lester. The teen is a straight-A student, class president, and technology whiz who has built his own computer from scratch. Lester and other young people with high potential are hosted by UCLA, given a guided tour of the campus, provided academic advice and financial aid information, and offered any other assistance and counseling they may need. Under Copeland-Morgan's tutelage, many young people of color have been inspired to attend UCLA. One of these was Lester. He says that after his tour of UCLA with other black males, he felt a sense of belonging. His teachers had suggested that he attend Stanford or Harvard, but Damion says, "UCLA is No. 1 on my list."

Quoted in Teresa Watanabe, "How UCLA Is Boosting Campus Diversity, Despite the Ban on Affirmative Action," *Los Angeles Times*, June 23, 2016. www.latimes.com.

"For too long, black people and other communities of color have faced barriers to access new technology and innovations," says NAACP official Derrick Johnson. "This groundbreaking partnership with Airbnb will help bring new jobs and economic opportunities to our communities."[79]

Perspectives on Racial Equality

Partnerships and other types of efforts can make a positive difference in fighting racial discrimination. One challenge, however, is that white people and people of color often disagree on how serious the problem of racial discrimination is—and even whether it exists at all. A Pew Research Center survey in October 2017 showed a pronounced disconnect between black and white perspectives on this issue. In one question, respondents were asked which was the bigger problem: people seeing discrimination where it really does not exist, or people not seeing discrimination where it really *does* exist. Among blacks, 84 percent chose the option of people *not* seeing discrimination when it was really there, and that was also the perspective of 66 percent of Hispanics. White people saw it differently; only 49 percent said that people do not see discrimination.

Similar differences in perspective were revealed during a Pew Research Center survey from 2016. Among people of color, 88 percent said the country needs to continue making changes for blacks to have equal rights with whites. Comparatively, 53 percent of white survey participants thought there was still work to do for blacks to achieve equal rights. Surprisingly, only a small percentage of black participants (43 percent) and white participants (40 percent) are confident that the country will eventually make the changes needed for blacks to have equal rights. "This gulf in optimism is incredibly troubling," says journalist Charles M. Blow. "What happens to a people when they stop believing, stop hoping, stop trusting that a concerted effort toward improvement will bear fruit?"[80]

"What happens to a people when they stop believing, stop hoping, stop trusting that a concerted effort toward improvement will bear fruit?"[80]

—African American journalist Charles M. Blow

A Long Way to Go

From efforts to improve relationships between community members and police to forming partnerships between businesses and civil rights groups, numerous efforts are underway to address racial discrimination. Individuals and organizations throughout the

United States are passionate about this issue and willing to work toward ending racial discrimination.

Yet even as progress has been made, and despite laws that prohibit racial discrimination, it remains a troubling and frustrating fact of life for people of color. They must continue to endure it, says African American producer and writer Terrance Heath, even when others may be blind to it. “Every week there’s some fresh reminder” that racial discrimination is far from being eliminated, says Heath. “Its nature can be interpersonal or institutional. It doesn’t always carry a sign, wave a confederate battle flag, or carry handcuffs. It may not even be consciously intended. It can be hard to pin down, and next to impossible to prove. . . . None of that makes the impact any less real.”[81]

SOURCE NOTES

Introduction: Perspectives on Racial Discrimination

1. Quoted in Merrit Kennedy, "Lead-Laced Water in Flint: A Step-by-Step Look at the Makings of a Crisis," NPR, April 20, 2016. www.npr.org.
2. Rasha Demashkieh et al., *The Flint Water Crisis: Systemic Racism Through the Lens of Flint*. Lansing, MI: Michigan Civil Rights Commission, 2017. www.michigan.gov.
3. Demashkieh et al., *The Flint Water Crisis*.
4. Anthony DiMaggio, "Why Black Lives Matter Won't Go Away: A Primer on Systemic Racism in America," *CounterPunch*, July 18, 2016. www.counterpunch.org.
5. Ryan Struyk, "Blacks and Whites See Racism in the United States Very, Very Differently," CNN Politics, August 18, 2017. www.cnn.com.

Chapter 1: The Years-Long Struggle for Equality

6. Quoted in Siobhan McAndrew, "Two Black Teens Face Racist Bullying in Yerington—and They Say No One Is Stopping It," *Reno (NV) Gazette Journal*, November 18, 2017. www.rgj.com.
7. Quoted in *Tolliver v. Lyon County School District*, US District Court, D. Nevada, 2018.
8. Quoted in *Tolliver v. Lyon County School District*.
9. Quoted in *Tolliver v. Lyon County School District*.
10. Quoted in McAndrew, "Two Black Teens Face Racist Bullying in Yerington—and They Say No One Is Stopping It."
11. David Pilgrim, "What Was Jim Crow?," Ferris State University Jim Crow Museum of Racist Memorabilia, 2012. https://ferris.edu.
12. Pilgrim, "What Was Jim Crow?"
13. Pilgrim, "What Was Jim Crow?"
14. Pilgrim, "What Was Jim Crow?"

15. Quoted in Chin Jou, "The Jim Crow North? Dining in New York City Before the Civil Rights Act of 1964," *Huffington Post*, September 23, 2014. www.huffingtonpost.com.
16. Earl Warren, *Brown v. Board of Education of Topeka*, 347 US 483, 1954.
17. Quoted in *Scholastic*, "Interview with Rosa Parks," 1997. http://teacher.scholastic.com.
18. Quoted in Melvin Banks, "Dr. King Stressed Nonviolence to Fight Injustice," Urban Faith, 2014. https://urbanfaith.com.
19. Martin Luther King Jr., "I Have a Dream," August 28, 1963. http://drmartinlutherking.net.
20. Barack Obama, "Remarks by the President at Memorial Service for Fallen Dallas Police Officers," White House, July 12, 2016. https://obamawhitehouse.archives.gov.

Chapter 2: Law Enforcement

21. James W. Buehler, "Racial/Ethnic Disparities in the Use of Lethal Force by US Police, 2010–2014," *American Journal of Public Health*, February 2017. http://ajph.aphapublications.org.
22. Quoted in David Gardner, "This Could Have Been Me," Bleacher Report, June 8, 2017. http://bleacherreport.com.
23. Quoted in Jolie McCullough, "Why the Murder Charge Against the Texas Police Officer Who Killed Jordan Edwards Is Rare," *Texas Tribune*, July 18, 2017. www.texastribune.org.
24. Quoted in Jaide Timm-Garcia et al., "Jordan Edwards' Killing Fuels Town's Grief—and a Call for Justice," CNN, May 6, 2017. www.cnn.com.
25. Redditt Hudson, "I'm a Black Ex-Cop, and This Is the Real Truth About Race and Policing," Vox, May 28, 2015. www.vox.com.
26. US Department of Justice, "Investigation of the Cleveland Division of Police," December 4, 2014. www.justice.gov.
27. Quoted in Rachel Clarke and Christopher Lett, "What Happened When Michael Brown Met Officer Darren Wilson," CNN, November 11, 2014. www.cnn.com.
28. US Department of Justice, "Investigation of the Ferguson Police Department," March 4, 2015. www.justice.gov.
29. Mark NeJame, "Trayvon Martin Shooting Wasn't a Case of Racial Profiling," CNN, May 30, 2012. www.cnn.com.
30. Quoted in *Harvard Gazette*, "Racial Discrimination Still Rules, Poll Says," October 30, 2017. https://news.harvard.edu.

31. DiMaggio, "Why Black Lives Matter Won't Go Away."
32. US Department of Justice, "Investigation of the Ferguson Police Department."
33. US Department of Justice, "Investigation of the Chicago Police Department," January 13, 2017. www.justice.gov.
34. Hudson, "I'm a Black Ex-Cop, and This Is the Real Truth About Race and Policing."

Chapter 3: Housing Discrimination

35. Quoted in Emily Sullivan, "Looking for a Home When Your Name Is Hispanic and Finding Discrimination Instead," NPR, November 2, 2017. www.npr.org.
36. Danielle Douglas-Gabriel, "Home Buying While Black," *Washington Post*, September 7, 2017. www.washingtonpost.com.
37. Douglas S. Massey, "The Legacy of the 1968 Fair Housing Act," *Sociology Forum*, June 2015. www.ncbi.nlm.nih.gov.
38. Quoted in Dmitri Mehlhorn, "A Requiem for Blockbusting: Law, Economics, and Race-Based Real Estate Speculation," *Fordham Law Review*, 1998. http://ir.lawnet.fordham.edu.
39. Quoted in Mehlhorn, "A Requiem for Blockbusting."
40. Dean Browning Webb, *RICO Conspiracy Law and the Pinkerton Doctrine*. Bloomington, IN: Xlibris, 2013, p. 90.
41. Lyndon B. Johnson, "Remarks Upon Signing the Civil Rights Act," American Presidency Project, April 11, 1968. www.presidency.ucsb.edu.
42. Massey, "The Legacy of the 1968 Fair Housing Act."
43. Quoted in Ari Shapiro, "'The Color of Law' Details How U.S. Housing Policies Created Segregation," NPR, May 17, 2017. www.npr.org.
44. Quoted in *Detroit Jewish News*, "Out-Migration to Suburbs Started in the 1950s, but Now Some Are Returning to the Urban Core," January 25, 2017. https://thejewishnews.com.
45. Shanti Abedin et al., *The Case for Fair Housing: 2017 Fair Housing Trends Report*. Washington, DC: National Fair Housing Alliance, 2017. http://nationalfairhousing.org.
46. Abedin et al., *The Case for Fair Housing*.
47. Julia Angwin and Terry Parris Jr., "Facebook Lets Advertisers Exclude Users by Race," ProPublica, October 28, 2016. www.propublica.org.
48. Quoted in Angwin and Parris, "Facebook Lets Advertisers Exclude Users by Race."

49. Julia Angwin et al., "Facebook (Still) Letting Housing Advertisers Exclude Users by Race," ProPublica, November 21, 2017. www.propublica.org.

Chapter 4: Employment and Education

50. Quoted in Hilary Hurd Anyaso, "Research Finds Entrenched Hiring Bias Against African-Americans," *Northwestern Now*, September 1, 2017. https://news.northwestern.edu.
51. Lincoln Quillian et al., "Meta-analysis of Field Experiments Shows No Change in Racial Discrimination in Hiring Over Time," PNAS, October 10, 2017. www.pnas.org.
52. Quillian et al., "Meta-analysis of Field Experiments Shows No Change in Racial Discrimination in Hiring Over Time."
53. Quoted in Lisa Nagele-Piazza, "Bass Pro to Pay $10.5 Million to Settle Hiring Discrimination Claims," Society for Human Resource Management, August 10, 2017. www.shrm.org.
54. Quoted in Nagele-Piazza, "Bass Pro to Pay $10.5 Million to Settle Hiring Discrimination Claims."
55. Quoted in Richard Connelly, "Bass Pro Shops Alleged Racism: The Five Worst Quotes from Managers," *Houston Press*, September 21, 2011. www.houstonpress.com.
56. Quoted in Nagele-Piazza, "Bass Pro to Pay $10.5 Million to Settle Hiring Discrimination Claims."
57. Equal Employment Opportunity Commission, "Harassment." www.eeoc.gov.
58. Quoted in Sam Levin, "Women Say They Quit Google Because of Racial Discrimination: 'I Was Invisible,'" *Guardian* (Manchester), August 18, 2017. www.theguardian.com.
59. Quoted in Levin, "Women Say They Quit Google Because of Racial Discrimination."
60. Quoted in Levin, "Women Say They Quit Google Because of Racial Discrimination."
61. Quoted in Levin, "Women Say They Quit Google Because of Racial Discrimination."
62. Quoted in Levin, "Women Say They Quit Google Because of Racial Discrimination."
63. Lyndon B. Johnson, "Commencement Address at Howard University: 'To Fulfill These Rights,'" American Presidency Project, June 4, 1965. www.presidency.ucsb.edu.
64. Quoted in Paul Rockwell, "Affirmative Action Triumphs: The Untold Stories," *In Motion Magazine*. www.inmotionmagazine.com.

65. Quoted in Rockwell, "Affirmative Action Triumphs."
66. Quoted in Scott Pelley, "Sotomayor on Role Affirmative Action Played in Her Life," CBS News, January 11, 2013. www.cbsnews.com.
67. Quoted in Pelley, "Sotomayor on Role Affirmative Action Played in Her Life."

Chapter 5: Efforts to End Racial Discrimination

68. Quoted in NPR, "Cops and Barbers: A Friendship Forged Between Blacks and Whites in Charlotte, NC," October 9, 2016. www.npr.org.
69. Rob Dance, "A Cop Walks into a Barbershop," Allegory Foundation, March 9, 2017. www.allegoryfoundation.org.
70. Quoted in NPR, "Cops and Barbers."
71. Quoted in NPR, "Cops and Barbers."
72. Quoted in NPR, "Cops and Barbers."
73. Quoted in NPR, "Cops and Barbers."
74. Brentin Mock, "What Police and Poor Communities Really Think of Each Other," *CityLab*, February 23, 2017. www.citylab.com.
75. Nancy La Vigne, Jocelyn Fontaine, and Anamika Dwivedi, "How Do People in High-Crime, Low-Income Communities View the Police?," Urban Institute, February 2017. www.urban.org.
76. Lida Shepherd, "WV Community Members, Police, Work Together to Address Racism," American Friends Service Committee, March 17, 2017. www.afsc.org.
77. Quoted in Katelyn Vue, "ThreeSixty Focus on . . . Medaria Arradondo," ThreeSixty, November 15, 2017. http://threesixtyjournalism.org.
78. Quoted in Olivia Solon, "Airbnb Host Who Canceled Reservation Using Racist Comment Must Pay $5,000," *Guardian* (Manchester), July 13, 2017. www.theguardian.com.
79. Quoted in Nick Staff, "Airbnb Teams Up with the NAACP to Fight Racism on Its Platform," Verge, July 26, 2017. www.theverge.com.
80. Charles M. Blow, "The State of Race in America," *New York Times*, June 30, 2016. www.nytimes.com.
81. Terrance Heath, "The GOP Can't Get off the Hook by Declaring the 'End' of Racism," Campaign for America's Future, December 9, 2013. http://ourfuture.org.

ORGANIZATIONS AND WEBSITES

American Civil Liberties Union (ACLU)
125 Broad St., 18th Floor
New York, NY 10004
website: www.aclu.org

The ACLU works with courts, legislatures, and communities to defend and preserve the rights and liberties that are guaranteed for all Americans under the US Constitution. Its website offers a number of articles, reports, and opinion pieces about racial discrimination.

Anti-Defamation League
823 United Nations Plaza
New York, NY 10017
website: www.adl.org

The Anti-Defamation League fights anti-Semitism and all forms of bigotry, defends democratic ideals, and protects civil rights for all. Its website offers a resource library with a wealth of articles and other publications about racial discrimination.

Century Foundation
One Whitehall St., 15th Floor
New York, NY 10004
website: https://tcf.org

The Century Foundation seeks to encourage opportunity, reduce inequality, and promote security at home and abroad. Its website's search engine produces numerous articles about racial discrimination and related issues.

National Association for the Advancement of Colored People (NAACP)

4805 Mt. Hope Dr.
Baltimore, MD 21215
website: www.naacp.org

The NAACP is the oldest and largest civil rights organization in the United States. Numerous publications related to racial discrimination can be found on the website.

Southern Poverty Law Center

400 Washington Ave.
Montgomery, AL 36104
website: www.splcenter.org

The Southern Poverty Law Center is dedicated to fighting hate and bigotry and to seeking justice for society's most vulnerable people. Its website's search engine produces articles, reports, and other publications about racial discrimination and related topics.

Vera Institute of Justice

233 Broadway, 12th Floor
New York, NY 10279
website: www.vera.org

The Vera Institute of Justice is an independent, nonpartisan organization dedicated to justice policy and practice. Its website offers a number of publications related to racial discrimination.

FOR FURTHER RESEARCH

Books

Kamal Al-Solaylee, *Brown: What Being Brown in the World Today Means (for Everyone)*. New York: HarperCollins, 2017.

Eduardo Bonilla-Silva, *Racism Without Racists*. Lanham, MD: Rowman & Littlefield, 2017.

Matthew Horace and Ron Harris, *The Black and the Blue: A Cop Reveals the Crimes, Racism, and Injustice in America's Law Enforcement*. New York: Hachette, 2018.

Ron Johnson, *13 Days in Ferguson*. Carol Stream, IL: Tyndale House, 2018.

Peggy J. Parks, *The Black Lives Matter Movement*. San Diego: ReferencePoint Press, 2018.

Beverly Daniel Tatum, *Why Are All the Black Kids Sitting Together in the Cafeteria?* New York: Basic Books, 2017.

Ken Wytsma, *The Myth of Equality*. Downers Grove, IL: InterVarsity, 2017.

Internet Sources

Shanti Abedin et al., *The Case for Fair Housing: 2017 Fair Housing Trends Report*. Washington, DC: National Fair Housing Alliance, 2017. http://nationalfairhousing.org/wp-content/uploads/2017/04/TRENDS-REPORT-4-19-17-FINAL-2.pdf.

Rochaun Meadows-Fernandez, "The Little Understood Mental-Health Effects of Racial Trauma," *The Cut* (blog), June 23, 2017. www.thecut.com/2017/06/the-little-understood-mental-health-effects-of-racial-trauma.html.

New York Times, "First Encounters with Racism," August 2, 2017. www.nytimes.com/2017/08/02/us/first-encounters-with-racism.html.

Brianna Sacks, "High Schools Are Dealing with Repeated Acts of Racism and Students Are Concerned," BuzzFeed News, October 23, 2017. www.buzzfeed.com/briannasacks/teens-at-these-high-schools-are-protesting-a-rise-in-racist.

Anita M. Samuels, "Social Media Has Become a Catalyst for the Spread of Racism and Hate," *New York Daily News*, February 9, 2017. www.nydailynews.com/news/national/social-media-catalyst-spread-racism-article-1.2967833.

Nick Statt, "Facebook Continues to Let Advertisers Racially Discriminate in Housing Ads," Verge, November 21, 2017. www.theverge.com/2017/11/21/16686524/facebook-housing-advertisements-discrimination-race.

INDEX

Note: Boldface page numbers indicate illustrations.